Classic
FRENCH
C·U·I·S·I·N·E

Edited by Rosemary Moon

SMITHMARK

ILLUSTRATIONS BY
CAMILLA SOPWITH AND LAWRIE TAYLOR

CLB 4367
© 1995 CLB Publishing

This edition published in 1995 by Smithmark Publishers, Inc.
16 East 32nd Street, New York NY 10016

SMITHMARK books are available for bulk purchase for sales promotion
and premium use. For details write or call the manager of special sales,
SMITHMARK Publishers, Inc.
16 East 32nd Street, New York,
NY 10016; (212) 532-6600

Produced by CLB Publishing
Godalming Business Centre
Woolsack Way, Godalming, Surrey, UK

ISBN 0-8317-1121-3

Printed in South Africa
10 9 8 7 6 5 4 3 2 1

CONTENTS

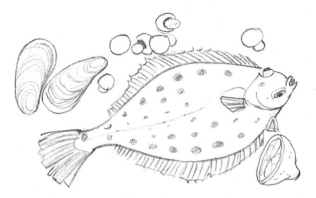

INTRODUCTION

What makes France the greatest nation of food lovers and cooks, the land of the premier cuisine of the world? The answer is perfectly simple – the French know and care about their food.

The Mediterranean Effect

I have a theory that the Mediterranean is a big influence on the general attitude of people toward food. Perhaps it is because the countries that border the Mediterranean all enjoy long hot summers, and people have to adapt their lifestyles to the heat of the day if they are to work, day in and day out, in such high temperatures. This means that life is taken at a more leisurely pace than in other, cooler climates; a good lunch might be enjoyed before a rest from the midday sun, then more work is undertaken before dinner, served late in the cool of the evening. Indeed lunch is still a big meal, if not the main meal, of the day in France – I have enjoyed several four-course midday meals in office dining rooms!

No Friday Night Supermarket Panic!
The French know and understand their food, and they are proud of it. If a meal takes a long time to prepare, so much the better – good food is more likely to be demanding on the cook than a hurriedly put together and quickly forgotten snack. That isn't to say that good food must always take hours to prepare but, if a meal is to be a simple celebration of fine ingredients, then time has to be spent in choosing and buying the food. A frantic trip around the supermarket on a Friday night, buying everything that is to be consumed by the household until the following Friday, will not allow for the loving preparation of meals that will satisfy and stimulate the family.

All Great Traditions Must Adapt
Perhaps, because I rather idolize the cooking of France and the dedication of the average Frenchman to the pleasures of the table, I am more than a little reluctant to acknowledge that attitudes toward food might be changing, even in the world center of fine cuisine. I have no doubt at all that things are changing in the cities, and that convenience foods are playing a larger and larger part in many homes where both parents work and there is a family to feed daily, and not that much time in which to do so. One has to hope that the convenience foods are of a high standard – but I am sure that they don't compare with home-cooked food. The most vital ingredient in any dish is love, and there's no way that the average food manufacturer can reproduce the tastes and textures achievable by someone cooking for family or friends.

What makes the country cookery of France so outstanding is that, through a dedication to the best foods available locally, the French have evolved a cuisine that is relatively simple and requires little in the way of modern kitchen wizardry to produce mouth-watering dishes.

Haute Cuisine and *Cuisine Bourgeoise*
Both have their place, but might become muddled in people's minds, especially if they think that all French cuisine is *haute*

cuisine. Haute cuisine is the stuff of banquets, of fine city restaurants, large châteaux and the ultimate dedication of life to the enjoyment of food and wine. It was a way of life for many in the late nineteenth and early twentieth centuries, but few of us can stand such indulgence now, because of our bank accounts, our hearts or our waistlines!

Such fine living is not the benchmark for the vast majority of French people – they derive their reputation for wonderful food through their regional and family inheritances of an outstanding appreciation of local ingredients, the ability to shop well and the tried and tested recipes of the generations that preceded them. It is this more simple culinary heritage, one which influences the vast majority of the French people, that truly earns France its reputation as the culinary center of the world.

From Seacoast Bistro to Routiers

The most wonderful thing to me about food in France today is that there is no snobbery attached to it. Everyone demands good food – the routier cafés frequented by long-distance truck drivers, serve food undreamed of on journeys on major roads in other countries. The French drivers simply would not return to a restaurant serving poor quality convenience food. The menu might include only a limited selection of dishes, but they are usually freshly prepared by skilled cooks producing honest food for the appreciation and enjoyment of others. The most outwardly uninspiring restaurant in a small village or country town will probably serve delightful meals at really affordable prices. And, if you don't want to cook yourself, where better to enjoy fresh seafood than at a harbor-side bistro?

Of course there are exclusive restaurants throughout France, many of them constantly busy. But who pays the inflated prices that these establishments charge? You are more likely to find them full of tourists if close to the fashionable resorts of the south, or expense account executives mingling with celebrities at chic restaurants in busy cities.

Regional Country Cookery

So many books have now been published on regional French cookery that it is easy to see how important this is to the cuisine of France. Of course there are recipes common throughout the country, but there are also regional variations and specialities.

Many areas cook extensively with wine – indeed it is really impossible to divorce food from wine when taking an overview of the French cuisine. The use of wine is influenced by its voluminous production – fine wines are produced virtually throughout the country with the exception of Normandy and Brittany, where cider-making is of greater importance. The local wines are used for many regional dishes – they have the right characteristics to mix with the local produce – why marinate local beef in a wine from a vineyard which is hundreds of miles away? The grape and the meat of the area will be made for each other, complementary ingredients for wonderful dishes.

Perhaps the current interest in French cookery stems from the fashion for more comforting foods – the return of homely puddings, and rich warming casseroles with hearty accompaniments? The French have always, in their regional dishes, managed to produce really satisfying fare from even the cheapest and toughest cuts of meat, cooking them slowly with plenty of vegetables, herbs and seasonings. This skill came through necessity in the days when the rich used only the best from any carcass and left the scraps for the servants. Time in those days was cheap – for many of us it is now a luxury.

The Culinary Regions of France

There are twelve principal culinary areas, although I sometimes get the feeling when I am in France that the district in which people live is almost as important as the whole region, but it is by the regions that most of us associate wines and foods.

What is grown and farmed locally will greatly influence the food of the region. Perhaps one of the best examples of this is the cooking of Normandy, which can be very rich as it is an area of dairy farming, of milk, cheese, butter and cream production. The shellfish found along the coast is also widely used, and the overall richness of the food is offset by the extensive use of apples in both sweet and savory dishes, for this is also the land of cider production. That said, Calvados, the apple brandy of the region, may easily obliterate all memories of what has gone before if served by too generous a host!

Every Region has its Own Specialty

I have already mentioned some of the specialty foods of Normandy. Others include the lambs which feed on the coastal salt marshes, and Salade Normande combining the best of all the local ingredients: apples, shellfish and cheeses.

Oysters and Artichokes

Brittany juts out into the Atlantic Ocean, and supports a very important fishing industry. Oysters, lobsters and salt cod are all specialties of Brittany, as are the huge globe artichokes and cauliflowers that are the pride of the region.

Where the north coast adjoins Normandy, the Bretons share with their neighbors a love of *"pré-salé"* salt marsh lamb. Brittany is also a land of crêpes and *galettes*, variations on a pancake theme which were eaten as staple foods when Brittany was isolated and unable to produce enough wheat for bread. Crêpes are now almost a fast food, available from stalls and small trailers in market places. As to my favorite Breton food, after the globe artichokes which I adore – well, it's the Gâteau Breton, a very buttery cake to be eaten by itself or with stewed fruits or mousses – delicious!

The Loire, Historical Nursery of France

The Loire valley is rich and fertile, producing top quality greengrocery. The Loire has been the nursery for many new fruits and vegetables introduced to France by explorers and traveling monarchs. King Charles VIII introduced Italian gardeners to Amboise, his Loire château, and they grew lettuces and peas. Indeed, there is a recipe for Petits Pois à la Française, where peas are actually cooked with shredded lettuce – it's different, delicious and well worth trying! Peaches, now one of the best and most prolific fruits in France, were also established in the Loire valley, and are extensively grown to this day, along with apricots, melons and pears.

Quenelles – a Fish Specialty

The Loire provides wonderful river fish – pike are still plentiful, and Quenelles de Brochet au Beurre Blanc, light spoonfuls of pike, poached and served in butter sauce, is a traditional dish of the Loire.

A Cathedral, Pâtés and a Tradition of Baking

These are the claims to fame of Chartres, the famous cathedral city in the north of the Loire region. When the monks were building the cathedral, much of the surrounding land was cleared to provide building materials, and this was then planted with wheat. The area, Beauce, became known as the granary of France. Chartres is also famed for its game pâtés – less acceptable is the local liking for lark pâté, something which I have no intention of trying.

Prunes, Oysters and Truffles

What a mixture! These foods all come from the south west, a region of which I have especially happy memories, for it was here that I first tasted French food prepared in a French home. In my early teens I set off on a concert tour of France with the local youth orchestra (in which I played the trumpet!). Our conductor had friends in a tiny village, and some eighty teenagers descended to give the first concert in the village church this century! Almost every house in the village had at least one British person staying there and, before the concert, we all ate cassoulet in the village square. Two days that triggered my life-long love of French food and customs!

A Profusion of Fish and Shellfish

The rivers of the south west offer excellent fish, but it is the Atlantic seaboard that has established the reputation of the area for fine oysters, scallops and saltwater crayfish. The oyster industry is centered on Arcachon, south of Bordeaux, where a huge, shallow bay provides an excellent breeding ground. The oysters take three years to reach a saleable size – a massive investment for the oyster farmers. Unfortunately, the farming yields slightly less flavorsome oysters than those able to grow in the wild. The Bordelais – the people of Bordeaux – often eat tiny sausages with their oysters (and, of course, they drink white wine with them!), which helps to give a little more flavor. Oysters raised at Marennes, north of Bordeaux, have more flavor and a quite distinctive greenish color – both characteristics are due to the algae present in the oyster beds.

Pruneaux d'Agen – the Finest Prunes in the World

The town of Agen on the Garonne is the center of the plum-growing area which produces the *pruneaux d'Agen*, huge moist prunes that I believe are the finest in the world. Most of the growers have their own drying ovens, and there is a heady sweetness in the air when the plums are being dried in late September.

The Secret of the Oak Woods

Truffles are a type of edible fungus, and the most famous truffle region in France is around Périgord and Quercy, where the highly prized black truffle is in season from November to March. They grow underground on the roots of oak trees, and are found by truffle hunters with pigs or dogs to help them – it is said that pigs are more efficient at hunting, but dogs are easier to discipline once a truffle has been located! Most truffles are canned, which prolongs their season but lessens their flavor. Only a slice or two is required to flavor any dish, as they can be somewhat pungent.

The Pyrenées and Gascony – a Spanish Influence

This region is tucked away on the Spanish border, and is greatly influenced by Spain. Bell peppers and olives are used extensively, and salt cod is popular – Brandade de Morue, a creamy paste of the preserved fish, is a local specialty.

Exotic Fish and Air-dried Hams

The Basque fishermen were great whalers but now the catch is mainly tuna, swordfish, sardines and anchovies. The Basque passion for spicy seasoning is reflected in their fish cookery – a local recipe for swordfish cooked with green peppercorns is included in the chapter on fish and seafood.

Named after the principal town of the region, jambons de Bayonne are air-dried, and then usually eaten raw, very thinly sliced. The hams have been renowned since the Middle Ages, and much of the special flavor comes from Espelette, the red peppers with which the hams are rubbed during curing. In some rural areas the number of hams hanging up to dry still gives an indication of the wealth of the household – you need to be able to afford the pigs in the first place!

Pickled in Armagnac!

Gascony adjoins the south western region of France, sharing a common border through the Armagnac-producing country. Much of the cooking of the area reflects an ancient tradition of food preservation, setting aside a store for consumption during the long, hard days of winter. Luxurious as fruits in Armagnac sounds to us, the tradition arose through the need to preserve the fruits for the winter months.

Confit – the Fat of the Land?

Confit is a method of preserving meats and poultry by salting and then cooking with fat. Goose fat is the most commonly used, and there are many geese in this area! The meat is usually preserved in large pieces that are cooked very slowly, totally covered in fat, until it is almost melting. When cold, the meat is covered in more melted fat, and then the *confit* is stored – it will keep for several months in the refrigerator.

Eat *confit* hot in a simple dish of beans or vegetables, frying it in its own fat until crispy. It may also be eaten cold in salads, and is considered to be one of the great delicacies of France.

Languedoc – Land of Roquefort, Garlic and Salt

Languedoc is the central southern region of France. Its main crop is wine and one department, the Hérault, produces one-fifth of the total wine of France! However, the three most important foods of the area are Roquefort, garlic and salt.

Roquefort, a pungent blue ewes' milk cheese, is the only cheese in France to have its own *appellation controllé*. It is matured for three months in the same limestone caves that have been used since 1411. It is now necessary to import sheep's milk from elsewhere to achieve a production of more than 27 million pounds a year.

Almost all the salt used in France is produced from the Salins du Midi, huge saltwater lakes in the Camargue. Most chefs and cooks prefer sea or rock salt for cooking, so it is no wonder that the French value this naturally produced seasoning.

Languedoc produces the best garlic in France. Garlic stalls are found in every market, and many towns and villages have annual garlic fairs. Vampires are seldom seen in this area! Garlic is supposed to be good for you, but too much may ruin your social life! Remember that sometimes just rubbing a cut clove around a salad bowl or over the surface of an ingredient will give all the flavor that is required.

Provence – a Little Province of Italy?

The Italian influence is clearly to be seen in the food of

Provence, so named as it was once a province of the Roman Empire. Tomatoes, garlic, herbs in plenty, olives, onions and anchovies combine with fish, vegetables and meat to offer a very varied, well flavored cuisine.

Olives and Olive Oil – a Provençal Way of Life

Provence is *the* main olive-producing area of France. Black olives are merely green olives that have been left to ripen for longer on the trees, but both are virtually inedible if eaten straight after picking. The olives have to be matured in lye, a strong alkaline solution, before they are ready for eating. The best are then packed in olive oil for sale.

Olive oil has become one of the most fashionable ingredients in contemporary cookery, and whole books have been written on the subject. Virgin and extra virgin oils, the purest varieties, are now easily produced, and are affordable, thanks to the introduction of centrifugal presses. A good olive oil, in my opinion, has a peppery finish and a good green color.

Franche-Comté and the Alps

This region borders both Italy and Switzerland, and is guarded by Mont Blanc. It is a mountainous region and home to some of the best wild mushrooms, walnuts and game in France.

Wild mushrooms are the perfect accompaniment to game, and, interestingly enough, often grow in good hunting areas. Care should be taken if you are a wild mushroom hunter – some are just not as edible as they look! In France most markets have a good selection of the mushrooms in season, and there is little necessity to find your own if you are not skilled in fungus recognition! It simply is not worth taking any risks as some varieties are deadly.

The fresh crop of walnuts each fall is an indication that winter is drawing in. Walnut oil is a delicious ingredient of salad dressings for special foods – I love it on avocados. It has helped to establish the walnut as a major crop – they were often grown as a secondary crop to supplement an income derived from vines, or vegetables. Walnuts are now valued for themselves, and justly so.

The French are great hunters, and many game birds have to be farmed to insure a regular supply for the table. Wild deer, rabbits and hare are common to this area and are hunted, as are small birds – a practise which I cannot condone.

Alsace-Lorraine, Home to Quiche and the Best *Foie Gras*

On a recent visit to Lorraine I was wondering what the locals ate apart from quiche! The answer was soft cheese and the most delicious hams and sausages, many of which clearly show a German influence.

Of course quiche is the best known dish of the region but the finest *foie gras* in France is also produced here.

Force-feeding – a Natural Inclination

The Romans used to force-feed geese on figs to enlarge their livers and produce *foie gras* – the French now achieve the same result by feeding with maize. The average person, and especially a non-foody, would condemn this as barbaric, but, although I have never actually seen the feeding done myself, except on television, various authorities have written that the geese actually seem to enjoy the feeding. It is true that geese are greedy and that they have always binged, especially before migration, so force-feeding is an extension of a natural tendency.

Foie Gras – the Delicacy

Throughout France *foie gras* is the gourmets' delight. Buying it is really a matter of luck as even the most experienced eye cannot detect which liver will dissolve away to a pan full of little more than juices when cooked for just a moment too long. Fresh is best, but color is no guide to quality as the livers vary from pink to a yellow ocher. The livers should be even in color, and cooked very lightly with next to no seasonings, allowing the delicate, slightly sweet flavor to dominate. Perhaps the best way to eat foie gras is with a slice of warm brioche, washed down with a glass of Sauternes or Champagne.

Champagne and the North

The cooking of this area is really very different from that of the rest of France, showing Belgian influence in the use of beer and an abundance of endive or chicory. Stews elsewhere are cooked in local wine, here carbonnades are popular, with the beef cooked in strong dark ale.

Chicory is often roasted with just a little onion, salt and pepper – I love it prepared like this as much of the bitter flavour, so strong in salads, is lost during cooking. Chicory is affordable in France – in England it is such a luxury – and it is always on my French shopping list! Vegetables are of prime importance to farmers in Champagne, and root vegetables in particular. It is one of the potato-growing areas and the French have a great tradition of producing tasty potatoes – those grown particularly for salads are amongst my favorites.

Of course, the main crop of Champagne is fizzy . . .

Little and Large in the Center of France

The central region of France is a vast mountainous area containing the Massif Central and the Auvergne, which is famed for its excellent blue cheeses. It is home to the Limousin cattle, which produce prime beef and veal. At the other end of the scale, it is also an area producing a great number of frogs – what happens to their bodies is a mystery to me as one is only ever offered the legs!

The cabbage is the symbol of the Auvergne, and it is widely used in the cooking of the area. Cabbage soup is a regional specialty, and the vegetable is often added to casseroles, or baked with small cuts of meat, especially pork.

My first memories of the central region are of Vichy, an elegant spa town producing the famous water. I have played my trumpet in the opera house, and it was in Vichy that I first tasted a proper vinaigrette – it was wonderful!

Last but not Least

The region of Burgundy and the Lyonnais may be last on my list, but it is the center of many of the great food trades of France and, of course, it is home to one of the greatest wine traditions of the world. Lyons is the center of the French charcuterie trade. The Lyonnais are also great lovers of chocolate and chestnuts, of prime quality around Lyons, which are often combined in sumptuous desserts. Snails, which are really an excuse for garlic butter in my opinion, are prized in Burgundy and *Escargots Bourguignons*, which are rather larger than other varieties of snail, are much prized. The cardoon, a relatively unknown vegetable outside France, looking like celery and having a flavor between a Jerusalem artichoke and fennel, is also grown here, and is best braised slowly over a low heat.

The Home of Coq au Vin

Poultry is very popular in Burgundy, and Coq au Vin, one of the greatest dishes of France, originates from here. Such a simple dish always sounds so impressive, yet all that is required, as for so much French cookery, are good ingredients in prime condition. Beef cooked in the red wine of the region, Boeuf Bourguignon, is also internationally acclaimed.

The Center of the World's Mustard Trade

Dijon, a relatively small town in the north of the region, produces over half the mustard consumed in the world! French mustard is considerably milder than English, and is used extensively with rabbit and also with kidneys – recipes for both are included in this book.

From even such a brief introduction to the culinary regions of France, you will begin to understand how deeply food is associated with French traditions. Many monasteries and religious centers developed cheeses and liqueurs, and experimented with spices and ingredients brought from abroad by explorers. Combinations of new ingredients and traditional foods grown in France led to a development of the French cuisine that, to this day, just hasn't stopped. Great traditions only survive in a healthy state if they are able to change and adapt, and French cooking has certainly done that! I have even included some new recipes in this book that I am certain are the classic French dishes of tomorrow!

The Vineyard of the World

Despite the huge variety of foods produced in France only 35 percent of the land is arable (24 percent is pasture or grazing for animals), and as few as 7 percent of the population are employed in agriculture. Included in the arable lands are the vineyards, which cover about 3.2 million acres and produce around 1.8 billion gallons of wine a year, making France and Italy jointly the largest wine producers in the world. France alone produces around one quarter of the world's wine.

I firmly believe that it is almost impossible to buy a really awful bottle of wine in France – perhaps the lowest quality wines are exported? I know that I have never had a bottle that was less than enjoyable when on French soil!

There are two distinct styles of wine produced; the *vin ordinaire* for everyday drinking, and the more specialised wines from the great châteaux which usually benefit from cellerage and maturation.

Country Wines and the Great Châteaux

Much of the *vin ordinaire* is produced in the south of France, and there has been a great effort recently to re-name it *vin du pays* (country wine) – this sounds more classy and somehow instantly makes the wine a little more expensive! These wines are generally best drunk as young as possible, and benefit from being consumed with food – they are characterful but often not particularly rounded, so local dishes from the southern regions of France, flavored with garlic, tomatoes, olives and other Mediterranean ingredients, do complement the wines particularly well.

To describe the great châteaux and fine wines of France adequately would require a whole bookful of space! Many fine wines have been auctioned for vast amounts of money – a 1794 bottle of Château d'Yquem was sold at Christies, London, for £36,000 in 1986, a positive bargain compared to a 1787 Château Lafite sold for £105,000 in the same year! Imagine opening it to find that it had gone off! I can't see the point in spending that sort of money on wine – I should also mention that I can't begin to contemplate having that sort of money to spend on wine! Suffice it to say that, whatever your taste and whatever your budget, the French have such an enormous and diverse wine industry that there will always be an excellent selection of wines to choose from, quite literally something to suit everyone.

The New World Challenge

Wine industries are now flourishing in many New World countries such as the United States, Australia and Chile, to name but a few. All are producing excellent wines, but I do find that they tend to be very similar, often using the same type of grapes. Of course, that is a sweeping statement, but Chardonnays and Cabernet Sauvignons do seem to crop up with amazing regularity. Within France there is such a variety of wine styles to choose from.

Investment in the New World has produced consistent quality at reasonable prices. Much of the wine comes from hi-tech wineries with vast gleaming stainless steel vats which seem centuries away from the oak barrels in romantic château cellars that are still common in France. However, the very strong challenge from the New World has been good for us, the consumers, by forcing the French to update their image, and pay greater attention to quality in all areas of their wine production. Care has always been lavished on the wines of the great châteaux, but the cost of such wines is prohibitive for the average enthusiast. The move to *vin du pays* has encouraged much better wines within even the lowest price range.

Two Great Names in French Cuisine

I really believe that the French are the best advertisement possible for their cuisine as they are so universally enthusiastic about eating and drinking! However, there are two names which really stand out in the history of French food, one a gastronome and one a chef.

Brillat-Savarin, the Gastronome

Jean Anthelme Brillat-Savarin was born in 1755, and died in Paris in 1826. Throughout his life he was an enthusiastic amateur in the world of food – his employment was as a magistrate and politician. His greatest work – *The Psychology of Taste* – was published a year before his death in 1825, and is a treatise on the art of cookery, combining observations, anecdotes and his sheer pleasure in eating. Many dishes were named after Brillat-Savarin, in recognition of all he did for the

French cuisine.

Auguste Escoffier, a Brilliant Chef

Escoffier was born in France in 1846, but it was abroad, in England, that he established himself as one of the greatest chefs of all time. He began cooking when he was twelve, and moved to London after six years in Paris and some time at the Grand Hotel in Monte Carlo.

Escoffier was the first chef at the Savoy Hotel, where he presided over the kitchens for eight years before moving on to the Carlton Hotel, then one of the leading hotels in London. He spent some time in Europe and the United States, collecting ideas for the 10,000 recipes with which he is credited. Escoffier certainly perfected many of the great sauces and culinary decorations still in use today. He was made a Chevalier of the Légion d'Honneur in 1920, and an Officier of the Légion in 1928.

Escoffier retired in 1921 at the age of 75, and then spent much of his time writing. He died, leaving an enormous legacy of creative genius, in 1935.

Bon Appétit!

Well, I've set the scene for a culinary tour of discovery, exploring just some of the classic dishes of France, the gastronomic capital of the world. I apologize if any of your favorites are not here, but I have tried to make a selection that covers the whole range of classic French cookery. Some standard recipes that are essential to many everyday dishes are included in a chapter of Basic Recipes at the end of the book.

There are two ingredients that I hope I have passed on to you and that are essential for creative French cookery: passion and enthusiasm. Bon appétit!

SOUPS & APPETIZERS

It is hard enough to know how to combine recipes into chapters for any cookbook, but when the book is about Classic French cookery, the most revered cuisine in the world, it is doubly difficult! "Soups & Appetizers" sound like an enormous chunk of recipes, but those contained within this chapter are suitable for serving as the first course of a meal or as cocktail canapés.

I have also included recipes for Anchoïade, Tapenade and Aïoli. These are pastes or dressings, and may be spread on toasts or croûtons, or added as an extra flavoring at the end of cooking – I love to stir a spoonful of tapenade into a daube just before serving. Pungent, savory and delicious – experiment with these foods if you have not yet discovered their delights! I quite often serve a selection of such sauces with a roasted bell pepper salad and olive oil bread as a dinner party appetizer.

Tasty – But Not Too Filling

Appetizers can be stunning either in their simplicity or in their elaborate and time-consuming preparation. The basic guideline is not to prepare anything which is too filling – the main course should be the focus of the meal. That said, many people find the appetizer to be the most enjoyable and memorable course, perhaps because it is the first food enjoyed on an empty stomach, or maybe because it makes the most impact on a freshly laid table.

Exotic Ingredients as Affordable Treats

Many of the more expensive ingredients, such as scallops, lobsters and asparagus, make excellent appetizers and can be enjoyed as such because they are affordable in small quantities! Shellfish are found in abundance around the coasts of Normandy and Brittany, both areas also rich in dairy produce which explains the classic serving of many of these foods in rich creamy sauces. When serving such luxurious foods hot, as an appetizer 'or as a main course, take great care not to overcook the shellfish. Purchased very fresh and in prime condition, shellfish requires very little cooking – overcooking will toughen and spoil these delectable foods.

I have included a number of salads which make perfect appetizers. One or two of these, such as Chicken Liver Salad, are served with the main ingredient freshly cooked and added to the salad while hot. Such salads have become very fashionable internationally in recent years, although they have been popular for a long time in France. I think they make an ideal appetizer, having always subscribed to the theory that a hot or warm appetizer immediately indicates that you have gone to considerable effort in the time-consuming preparation of the meal that follows. Of course, this need not be so, and a warm salad provides a delicious and effective illusion!

Soups as First Courses

Soups, once the main course or, indeed, the only course in the average family meal, are now first courses, a celebration of fresh vegetables in season, and a warming dish to serve before a main course of cold meats or fish. Canned soups may be a reliable stand-by for the typical summer's day away from the south of France, when high temperatures and brilliant sunshine are not always as reliable as they might be, but soup should not only be thought of as emergency heating! I find that the best soups are made from vegetables and other ingredients when they are in season and full of flavor. Lobster Bisque and Crab Soup are both delicious treats, but perfectly affordable to make when there is a glut of shellfish.

Soup Kitchens and Restaurants

It should be remembered that soups actually gave rise to the modern restaurant as the center of good food. The very first eating establishment to be known as a restaurant was founded in Paris in 1765 by a French soup maker, who sold a selection of soups or restoratives from his upmarket soup kitchen. This became known as a restaurant, because of the restorative nature of his dishes. So much in the world of food has its origins in France! The French are still great soup-eaters, and many country folk do not consider that they have had a meal, even in the summer, if it has not been preceded by a plate of soup. Perhaps the habit of still serving soup in proper soup plates, rather than in all-purpose bowls, indicates the importance of soup in France?

When planning the first course of your meal, the most important thing to consider is the provision of a contrast to the course that follows, both in flavor and texture. Having satisfied that criteria, indulge yourself!

FRENCH ONION SOUP

I have read more than once that this soup was traditionally consumed in the small hours, after a heavy night on the town! Whether or not that is true, it is certainly one of the best known classic soups of France. The secret of a good onion soup is to get as much color as possible from the onions by browning them well.

Serves 6

INGREDIENTS
½ cup butter
6 large onions, thinly sliced
2 cloves garlic, crushed
Salt and freshly ground black
   pepper
6 tablespoons red wine
5 cups well-flavored stock
6 slices French bread, toasted
1 cup finely grated Gruyère
   cheese

Melt the butter in a large pan. Add the onion and garlic, and cook over a low heat for about 30 minutes, stirring ocasionally to prevent them from sticking to the pan. Season with salt and pepper. Add the wine, and boil until slightly reduced. Add the stock, and bring the soup to a boil, stirring continuously. Reduce the heat, and simmer for 30 minutes. If the soup becomes too thick, stir in a little extra stock or water.

Serve the soup in individual bowls. Float a slice of toast in each bowl, and scatter with the grated cheese. Place under a hot broiler for a few minutes to melt and brown the cheese.

PEASANT'S SOUP

Cabbages are widely used in France, so it is no surprise to find this vegetable in a soup! Such country fare derives its richness from a little bacon and some drippings from either a goose or a duck. Once a staple in almost every larder, these ingredients are now luxuries, and, if not available, should be replaced with 2–3 tablespoons of well-flavored olive oil.

Serves 6

INGREDIENTS
1½ cups shredded cabbage
2 tablespoons goose or other poultry drippings
1 cup chopped, smoked bacon
1½ cups chopped leeks
1 turnip, peeled and diced
5 cups chicken stock
1¾ cups peeled and diced potatoes
6 slices of bread
Salt and freshly ground black pepper

Blanch the cabbage in a large pan of boiling water for 3 minutes. Drain and set the cabbage aside, discarding the water. Melt the drippings in the pan. Add the bacon, and cook over a low heat – do not let the bacon brown. Stir in all the vegetables except the cabbage and potatoes, and cook over a low heat for a few minutes. Add the blanched cabbage to the pan, then pour in the stock. Bring to a boil. Cover the soup, and simmer very slowly for about 90 minutes – the long, slow cooking time will really let the flavors of the vegetables blend together and develop. Add the potatoes for the last 20 minutes of the cooking time. If the stock reduces too much during cooking, add a little extra water.

Place a slice of fresh bread in the bottom of each individual soup bowl. Season the soup to taste with salt and pepper, and ladle the soup into the bowls, over the bread. Serve immediately.

LEEK AND POTATO SOUP

This popular soup combines two favorite ingredients. In the winter it is a warming, comforting dish. In the summer, when made with young, tender vegetables, it can be puréed, chilled, and then, with the addition of cream, it becomes the classic Vichyssoise.

Serves 4-6

INGREDIENTS
2 tablespoons butter
4 large leeks, thinly sliced
4 large potatoes, peeled and diced
5 cups chicken stock
2½ cups water
Salt and freshly ground black pepper
4 tablespoons heavy cream

To Serve
2 tablespoons softened butter
4 tablespoons light cream
1 tablespoon freshly chopped parsley
1 tablespoon freshly chopped chives

Melt the butter in a large pan. Add the prepared leeks, and cook them over a low heat until softened but not browned. Add the potatoes, stock, water, salt and pepper, and bring to a boil. Cover the pan, and simmer for about 35 minutes, until all the vegetables are cooked.

Stir the heavy cream into the soup, and season it to taste. Serve the soup as it is, or purée in a blender or food processor. Serve dotted with the remaining butter, and with the light cream swirled into the soup. Sprinkle with the freshly chopped herbs at the last minute.

PISTOU SOUP

Pistou is a delicious sauce of fresh basil and garlic. It differs from its Italian cousin pesto inasmuch as it often contains tomato but no pine nuts. The soup should be served piping hot with the sauce in a separate small bowl. Each person then stirs a spoonful of sauce into their soup before eating.

Serves 8

INGREDIENTS

1¼ cups lima beans, or small white beans, soaked overnight and drained
2 carrots, diced
2 zucchini, trimmed and diced
1 stalk celery, trimmed and sliced
1 pound thin green beans
2 leeks, white parts only, finely sliced
1 large onion, finely sliced
1 large potato, sliced
5 pints chicken stock
Bouquet garni
Salt and freshly ground black pepper

Pistou
6 cloves garlic
20-30 fresh basil leaves, depending on size
3 tomatoes, skinned, seeded and chopped
¾ cup freshly grated Parmesan cheese
½ cup olive oil

Rinse the soaked beans, and cook them in a large pan of fresh water for 30 minutes, until just beginning to soften. Drain the beans, and then return them to the pan. Add the carrots, zucchini, celery, green beans, leeks, onion and potato, then the stock, bouquet garni, and salt and pepper. Bring the soup to a boil; reduce the heat and cover the pan, then simmer for 30-40 minutes, until the vegetables and the beans are cooked through and softened.

Make the Pistou while the soup is cooking. Pound the garlic, basil leaves and tomatoes together in a pestle and mortar. Stir in the cheese, and slowly add the olive oil, a little at a time, beating continuously until the mixture is smooth. The sauce can also be made in a blender or food processor, if preferred. Season with salt and pepper.

Season the soup, and serve with the pistou handed separately.

CREAM OF CAULIFLOWER AND PARSLEY SOUP

Madame du Barry, a contemporary of Louis XV, had a classic creamy cauliflower soup named after her. This soup is a variation on that classic dish, adding a generous flavoring of parsley. Use the French flat-leaf parsley if you can – it is easy to grow, and is also available in many large supermarkets in the fresh herbs section. You may prefer to use white pepper for this soup as it is more delicate in flavor than black.

Serves 6

Ingredients
¼ cup butter
8 ounces leeks, white parts only, cut into thin slices
5 cups chicken stock
1 pound cauliflower flowerets, washed and chopped
About 5 tablespoons, flat-leaf parsley
Scant 1 cup heavy cream
Salt and pepper

Melt half of the butter in a large pan, and cook the leeks until softened but not browned. Add the stock and the cauliflower. Stir well, and bring to a boil. Reduce the heat, and simmer the soup for about 30 minutes, until the cauliflower is just cooked. Reserve ⅔ cup of the soup, and purée the remainder in a blender or food processor. Rinse the pan, and return the soup to it.

Blanch the parsley in boiling, salted water for 1 minute, then drain well. Mix the parsley with the reserved cauliflower soup, and purée in a blender or food processor. Reheat the soup if necessary, and stir in the cream and the remaining butter, in small pieces, then season well. Serve the cauliflower soup in individual bowls, swirling a spoonful of the blended parsley into each.

SOUPE DE POISSONS PROVENÇALE

France is famed for its fish soups which vary from smooth, creamy broths to robust mixed fish soups, some of which are almost a stew and a meal in themselves! This soup has the rich flavors of Provence, and is accompanied by rouille, a rich hot sauce of red bell peppers and olive oil.

Serves 4

INGREDIENTS

Soup
1 large onion, chopped
2 leeks, chopped
⅔ cup olive oil
2 cloves garlic, crushed
2 × 14-ounce cans chopped
  tomatoes
3 pounds mixed white fish
8 ounces shrimp or scampi
1 bay leaf
1 sprig thyme
1 small piece of fennel or 2 stalks
  parsley
1 strip orange rind
7½ cups water
⅔ cup dry white wine
2 pinches saffron strands
Salt and freshly ground black
  pepper
Tomato paste
¼ cup all-purpose flour
2 tablespoons butter
Light cream

Sauce Rouille
1 small red chili
½ cup chopped red bell pepper
  or canned pimento
3-4 tablespoons fresh white
  bread crumbs
3 cloves garlic, crushed
1 egg yolk
Salt and freshly ground black
  pepper
⅔ cup extra virgin olive oil

To Serve
Grated Parmesan cheese
Croûtons

Prepare the soup. Cook the chopped onion and leeks in the olive oil until softened but not browned. Add the garlic with the tomatoes, then bring the mixture to a boil. Cook over a low heat for 5 minutes while preparing the fish. Fillet and skin the fish, cutting it into large pieces. Shell the shrimp or scampi, and tie the bay leaf, thyme, fennel and orange peel together with a piece of string. Add the prepared fish and aromatics to the tomato mixture with the water, wine, saffron, salt and pepper. Simmer, uncovered, for 30-40 minutes.

Prepare the Sauce Rouille. Seed the chili, and chop it finely – only use half if you prefer a milder flavor. Chop the red bell pepper or pimento. Soak the bread crumbs in a little water; then squeeze them dry and put into a blender or food processor with the chili, bell pepper, garlic and egg yolk. Season with salt and pepper, and then blend to a smooth paste. This mixture may also be worked together with a pestle and mortar. Gradually add the olive oil in a thin, steady stream until the sauce has the consistency of mayonnaise.

Remove the bundle of herbs from the pan of soup, then purée the soup in a blender or food processor. Strain the soup if necessary, then season and add a little tomato paste for color. Rinse the pan, return the soup to it, and bring it to a boil. Mix the flour and butter together, and add to the soup a little at a time, whisking and boiling the soup between each inclusion. The soup should have the consistency of heavy cream. Stir a little light cream into the soup just before serving.

Spoon a little of the Sauce Rouille into each individual bowl of soup, and serve garnished with Parmesan and croûtons.

PUMPKIN SOUP

Pumpkins have always been in demand in the United States and France. They mature in the fall, making this soup ideal for serving before a main course of the new season's game. Drain the pumpkin well, otherwise the soup will be watery.

Serves 6

INGREDIENTS
3 pounds pumpkin, peeled and cut into cubes
1¼ cups milk
1¼ cups heavy cream
1 teaspoon ground cinnamon
Salt and freshly ground black pepper

Cook the pumpkin in boiling salted water until tender; this will take about 20 minutes. Drain the pumpkin well, and mash it with a fork until smooth. Put the pumpkin into a blender or a food processor with the milk, and purée.

Rinse the pan, and return the soup to it. Stir in the cream and cinnamon, and reheat the soup until almost boiling. Season well, and serve hot.

CHICKEN BREAST SALAD

For the best and most eye-catching presentation of this salad, use corn-fed chicken breasts – the meat is a most wonderful golden yellow color and looks stunning when combined with the avocado, lettuce and tomato. Many chickens are fed on corn in France to improve the flavor of the meat. This appetizer is quite filling, so serve it before a light main course, or as a light lunch dish.

Serves 6

INGREDIENTS
Knob of butter
3 corn-fed chicken breasts
⅔ cup dry white wine
¾ cup chicken stock
⅓ cup heavy cream
Salt and freshly ground black
  pepper
4 tomatoes
2 avocados, peeled, pitted and
  sliced
Juice of 1 lemon
Mixed salad greens for serving

Melt the butter in a skillet and quickly seal the chicken on all sides. Add the white wine to the skillet, and cook quickly until reduced by half. Pour in the stock, and cook over a medium heat until reduced by half. Reduce the heat to as low as possible; cover the pan, and cook for an additional 10-12 minutes, or until the chicken is cooked through. Remove the chicken breasts, and keep them warm. Return the pan to the heat, and stir in the cream, seasoning with salt and pepper. Bring to a boil, stirring continuously, and continue to boil until the sauce has thickened.

Skin and seed two of the tomatoes, then cut them into thin sticks and dice them. Cut the remaining tomatoes into thin slices.

Alternate slices of tomato and avocado, tossed in the lemon juice, around a bed of prepared salad greens on a serving plate. Slice the chicken breasts, and arrange them in the middle. Scatter with the diced tomato, and pour the sauce over the salad.

FISHERMAN'S SALAD

A new dish, an elegant appetizer on any occasion. Care must be taken in the preparation of the vegetables, but the stunning result makes it well worth the effort.

Serves 6

INGREDIENTS
1 carrot, scraped
½ cucumber, wiped, peeled and seeded
1 red bell pepper, seeded
1 zucchini, wiped
40 small shrimp, shelled (retain the peelings)
1 tablespoon olive oil
1 tablespoon brandy or Cognac
¾ cup light cream
Juice of ½ a lemon
2 tablespoons freshly chopped chervil

Cut each of the vegetables carefully into very fine julienne strips. As you finish each vegetable, put the strips in the refrigerator to keep them crisp and fresh. Fry the shrimp peelings in the olive oil briskly over a high heat for 5 minutes. Add the brandy or Cognac, and flambé the mixture. Let the alcohol burn out, then stir in the cream, and continue cooking over a low heat for about 10 minutes.

Press the sauce through a fine strainer, discarding all but the smooth sauce. Blend the sauce with a hand mixer, then put the sauce in the refrigerator to cool.

On a serving dish, spread a single layer of the vegetable strips and sprinkle over the shelled shrimp. Add the lemon juice to the cooled sauce, stir well and pour it over the salad. Sprinkle over the chervil, and serve.

CHICKEN LIVER SALAD

I have always associated chicken livers with France and French cookery, possibly because my first introduction to them was in a Pâté Maison, a smooth chicken liver pâté flavored with brandy and set with lots of creamy butter. This salad includes warm pan-fried livers and a warm dressing, added to the salad at the last moment – very chic!

Serves 4-6

INGREDIENTS
2 large globe artichokes
Juice of 1 lemon
Knob of butter
⅔ cup olive oil
12 ounces chicken livers
1 small onion, finely chopped
Mixed salad greens
4 tablespoons red wine vinegar
Salt and freshly ground black
   pepper

Prepare the artichokes by removing the stalks and then cutting off all the outer leaves with a small, sharp knife. Cook the artichokes with the lemon juice in boiling salted water until tender, about 15-20 minutes. Remove and discard the hairy chokes, and slice the remaining artichoke hearts.

Melt the butter in a skillet. Add 2 tablespoons of the olive oil, and cook the livers and onion over a medium high heat for about 5 minutes. Arrange the prepared salad greens on individual plates while the livers are cooking. Deglaze the skillet with 1 tablespoon of the vinegar, stirring it into the pan over a high heat and scraping up any pieces of livers from the bottom of the pan. Cook for a further 1-2 minutes, then arrange the livers on the salad greens, and top them with slices of the artichoke.

Warm the remaining vinegar in the skillet, and add the remaining oil. Season and whisk the dressing together until well blended. Pour a little of the warm dressing over each individual salad.

SMOKED HERRING SALAD

A nouvelle cuisine recipe especially developed for the sophisticated dinner party. Smoked salmon could be used in place of the smoked herring, if preferred.

Serves 6

INGREDIENTS
3 heads endive, wiped
4 smoked herring, filleted
4 large new potatoes, cooked
1 onion, finely chopped
8 cilantro seeds
1 teaspoon sea salt
⅔ cup olive or corn oil
1 teaspoon mustard
1 tablespoon wine vinegar
Pepper

Separate the endive leaves, and slice them lengthwise into thin strips. Slice the herring fillets crosswise, and mix with the endive leaves. Dice the potatoes, mix with the above, and add the onion, coriander seeds and salt.

In a salad bowl, mix together the oil, mustard, vinegar and pepper. Add all the other ingredients, and mix well to incorporate the sauce, or arrange on serving plates and drizzle over the dressing.

LAMB'S SWEETBREAD SALAD

You will have to find a friendly traditional butcher in order to obtain the sweetbreads for this recipe.

Serves 4

INGREDIENTS
12 ounces lamb's sweetbreads
Salt and freshly ground black
  pepper
1 tablespoon all-purpose flour
1 teaspoon sherry vinegar, or
  good quality red wine vinegar
2 tablespoons mayonnaise
1 tablespoon chicken stock
1 teaspoon freshly chopped
  chervil
1 crisp lettuce, broken into small
  pieces
2 tablespoons butter

Blanch the sweetbreads in boiling water for 1 minute; then drain and remove and discard the nerves. Chop the sweetbreads into small pieces. Season with salt and pepper, and coat in the flour.

Stir the vinegar into the mayonnaise, then stir in the stock – this should give a slightly thickened sauce. Stir in the chervil, and season with salt and pepper. Arrange the lettuce on individual serving plates.

Sauté the sweetbreads in the butter for 2-3 minutes, or until golden; then drain and arrange them on the prepared lettuce. Pour the chervil sauce over the sweetbreads, and serve immediately.

CHICKEN & WALNUT SALAD

A light and elegant salad – use whatever cheese you prefer, according to the flavors of the rest of the meal. I usually choose a ripe Brie, a Bleu d'Auvergne or a Pont l'Evêque. Replace the chicken with shellfish, and you almost have the classic Salade Normande.

Serves 6

INGREDIENTS
1 green apple, diced
1 red apple, diced
Juice of 1 lemon
1 pound cooked chicken breasts
1 cup shelled walnuts
1½ cups diced or crumbled
   cheese
Mixed salad greens

Dressing
½ cup yogurt
1 tablespoon Dijon mustard
½ cup olive oil
2 tablespoons white wine vinegar
2 tablespoons ground walnuts
Salt and freshly ground black
   pepper

Dice the apples, and toss them in the lemon juice to prevent them from discoloring. Cut the chicken breasts into neat cubes, and mix with the apple and shelled walnuts; then carefully mix in the cheese.

Mix the ingredients for the dressing together in a bowl, or shake well in a screw-topped jar. Season the dressing to taste, and pour it over the chicken and apple mixture.

Place a little salad on 6 small serving plates, top with the chicken, and serve immediately with fresh, crusty French bread.

HERBY GOAT CHEESE

Goat cheese is very popular in France, and many small farmers make their own cheeses to sell in the local markets. This recipe uses small soft cheeses – a soft cheese from a tub would be more appropriate than a mold-ripened cheese.

Serves 4

INGREDIENTS

2 fresh goat cheeses, weighing about 8 ounces in total
1 tablespoon finely chopped onion
1 tablespoon finely chopped shallot
1 tablespoon freshly chopped mixed herbs, such as chives, parsley and chervil
10 capers
5 peppercorns
Salt and freshly ground black pepper
Few drops vinegar
A squeeze of lemon juice
½ teaspoon olive oil

Mix the cheeses with the onion, shallot and freshly chopped herbs; then mix in the capers, peppercorns and the salt and pepper. Stir in the vinegar, lemon juice and olive oil, and mix well.

Divide the cheese between 4 small ramekins, pushing it down well, and then chill for about 2 hours. Turn out just before serving onto a bed of fresh salad greens.

HADDOCK MOUSSE

A deliciously light fish mousse in the new style of French cookery. This recipe may not be an established classic, but it soon will be! Serve the haddock mousse with a light dressing of olive oil, lemon juice, salt and pepper. Leaf gelatin dissolves more readily than the powdered variety – seek it out if you possibly can.

Serves 4

INGREDIENTS
3 leaves gelatin
3 small fillets of smoked haddock
1¼ cups fish stock
1 cup less 2 tablespoons heavy
 cream
1 tablespoon freshly chopped
 chives
Salt and freshly ground black
 pepper

Soak the gelatin in a bowl of cold water. Cut one of the haddock fillets in half, and chop it finely. Use either a very sharp knife or a food processor.

In a saucepan, heat the fish stock and the chopped haddock fillet over a low heat. Drain the gelatin sheets, and stir into the stock until they have completely dissolved. Remove from the heat, transfer to a clean bowl, and put into the refrigerator.

Meanwhile, whip the cream until it becomes light and fluffy. Keep cool. When the stock is completely cool, gently fold in the whipped cream, chives, salt and pepper. Return the mixture to the refrigerator for at least 2 hours.

Cut the remaining fillets into very thin slices, like smoked salmon, and spread them out slightly overlapping in 4 matching rectangles onto pieces of plastic wrap. Place spoonfuls of mousse across the center of each. There should be some mousse left over. Using the plastic wrap to help you, gently roll up the slices of haddock to make neat rolls. Put the rolls back into the refrigerator until ready to serve.

Using a teaspoon, form the remaining mousse into small oblong shapes, and serve with the haddock roll. Remove the plastic wrap before serving.

PÂTÉ DE CAMPAGNE

*A rough country-style pâté, there must be literally thousands
of variations on this recipe. The local wine or brandy, the
herbs and the seasonings all add their own particular touch.
Pâté de campagne, country pâté, is made throughout
France. Serve with hot toast and a salad garnish.*

Serves 10

INGREDIENTS
12 ounces pig's liver, skinned
  and tubes removed
3 cups coarsely ground pork
1 cup coarsely ground veal
2 cups coarsely ground pork fat
2 shallots, finely chopped
1 clove garlic, crushed
3 tablespoons Cognac
½ teaspoon ground allspice
Salt and freshly ground black
  pepper
1 teaspoon freshly chopped
  thyme or sage
10 slices bacon, rind and bones
  removed
2 tablespoons heavy cream
1 cup smoked ham, cut into ¼-
  inch cubes
1 large bay leaf

Preheat the oven to 350°F. Place
the liver into a food processor,
and process once or twice to
chop it roughly. Add the minced
meats and fat, shallots, garlic,
Cognac, allspice, salt and pepper,
and thyme, and process once or
twice to mix. Do not overwork
the mixture; it should be coarse.
You could chop the liver by
hand, and mix the pâté in a
bowl, if preferred.

Stretch the slices of bacon with
the back of a knife, and use to
line a terrine, metal loaf pan or
ovenproof glass dish. Stir the
cream and the ham into the meat
mixture by hand, then press it
into the prepared dish on top of
the bacon. Place the bay leaf on
top of the pâté, and fold over
any overlapping edges of bacon.

Cover the dish with a tight-fitting
lid or two layers of foil, and
place the dish in a bain marie (a
roasting pan of hand-hot water);
the water should come halfway
up the sides of the terrine. Bake
for 2 hours, or until the meat
juices run clear.

Remove the pâté from the oven
and take off the lid or foil. Cover
with fresh foil, and press the pâté
with heavy cans or balance scale
weights. Let cool at room
temperature, and then refrigerate,
still weighted, until completely
chilled and firm.

To serve, remove the weights
and foil. Turn the pâté out onto a
serving plate, and scrape off any
excess fat. Slice and serve.

CHICKEN LIVER PÂTÉ WITH CORIANDER

A variation on Pâté Maison, a popular chicken liver pâté made throughout France. Most people have their own way of seasoning the pâté – coriander is a most unusual and delicious flavoring. Serve with freshly made toast, or fresh crusty bread and a glass of the local wine.

Serves 4

INGREDIENTS
1 pound chicken livers, trimmed
1 cup softened butter
4 shallots, finely chopped
2 plump cloves garlic, chopped
2 teaspoons ground cilantro
2 teaspoons freshly chopped
    parsley
Salt and freshly ground black
    pepper
2 teaspoons mango chutney
Cilantro leaves and clarified
    butter to garnish

If the livers are large, cut them into smaller pieces. Melt half the butter in a skillet and add the shallots, garlic, ground coriander and livers. Cook together over a moderate heat for about 5 minutes, until the livers are cooked through. Let cool completely, then purée in a blender or food processor until smooth. Press the mixture through a metal strainer if a totally smooth pâté is required. Add the remaining butter, parsley, salt and pepper, and chutney. Process again until smooth, and transfer to a serving dish. Coat with clarified butter, and garnish with cilantro leaves when the butter has set. Chill for 2 hours, then serve with toast.

SPINACH & CHICKEN TERRINE

A lightly baked terrine, a variation on the classic Pâté de Campagne, but made with chicken. I like to serve such terrines with a thin homemade mayonnaise, lightly spiced with green peppercorns.

Serves 4-6

INGREDIENTS

8 ounces chicken breasts, boned and skinned
2 egg whites
2 cups fresh white bread crumbs
Salt and freshly ground black pepper
1 pound spinach, washed
3 tablespoons freshly chopped chervil, chives and tarragon, mixed
1¼ cups heavy cream
½ cup finely chopped walnuts
Nutmeg
Fromage blanc or low-fat cream cheese mixed with milk to a piping consistency

Preheat the oven to 325°F. Blend the chicken, 1 egg white, half the bread crumbs, salt and pepper in a food processor until well mixed. Cook the spinach in the water that clings to the leaves after washing for 3 minutes, or until just wilted. Remove the chicken from the food processor, and rinse the processor bowl.

Put the spinach into the processor with the herbs, the remaining egg white and the bread crumbs, salt, pepper and nutmeg. Process until well mixed. Mix half the cream with the chicken mixture and half with the spinach. Add the walnuts to the spinach with the cream.

Line a 9 × 5-inch loaf pan with baking parchment, and spread the chicken mixture evenly over the bottom of the pan. Cover with the spinach mixture, and carefully smooth the top. Cover with greased foil, sealing tightly. Place the pan in a dish, and add enough warm water to come halfway up the sides of the pan. Bake for 1 hour, or until firm. Let the terrine cool, then chill overnight.

Carefully lift the chilled terrine out of the pan using the lining paper. Peel off the paper, and place the terrine on a serving plate. Beat the cheese until smooth, adding milk as necessary to give a piping consistency, and pipe lines or a lattice over the top of the terrine. Serve sliced.

SNAILS WITH POTATOES IN NUTMEG

This is a completely new way of serving snails – a great dish to delight guests at your next dinner party. This dish is ready to serve as soon as the potatoes are cooked.

Serves 4

INGREDIENTS
8 medium potatoes
Light cream
Freshly grated nutmeg
Salt and freshly ground black
  pepper
40 canned snails, cooked and
  rinsed

Peel the potatoes and cut them into even slices. Blanch them for 30 seconds in lightly salted boiling water, then drain well. Put the potatoes into a skillet, add the cream, nutmeg to taste, salt and pepper. Add the snails, and cook over a low heat until the potatoes are quite tender.

When the potatoes are cooked, arrange them in a rose pattern with the snails in the middle and the cream sauce poured over.

CREAMED SPINACH

These delicious ramekins of spinach somehow manage a richness of flavor combined with mouth-watering lightness. The French for spinach is "épinard" – it is a very popular vegetable in France, and one which you will often come across on restaurant menus and in the descriptions of the dishes. Always use freshly grated nutmeg with spinach – they were made for each other!

Serves 6

INGREDIENTS
2¼ pounds spinach, cooked and well drained
5 eggs
1 cup heavy cream
Salt and freshly ground black pepper
Pinch of nutmeg
2 tablespoons butter

Preheat the oven to 300°F. Squeeze out any excess water from the spinach with your fingers, then place the spinach in a mixing bowl. Beat in the eggs, one at a time. Add the cream, salt, pepper and nutmeg, and mix well.

Grease 6 ramekin dishes with the butter, and spoon in the spinach mixture. Place the ramekins in a high-sided roasting pan, and pour in water to come halfway up the sides of the ramekins. Bake them for about 40-50 minutes, until the mixture is set. Serve hot.

OMELETTE ROUSSILLON

The wine-growing area of Roussillon is centered on the town of Perpignan in the southwest of France, close to the Spanish border. The Spanish influence is obvious in this tasty omelet, flavored with bell peppers and tomatoes. Omelet-making is an art – overcooking will make the eggs rubbery and tough.

Serves 1

INGREDIENTS

3 eggs
Salt and freshly ground black
   pepper
1 tablespoon butter
¼ green bell pepper, cut into
   small dice
2 ounces ham, cut into small dice
2 tomatoes, skinned, seeded and
   roughly chopped

Break the eggs into a bowl, and season with salt and pepper. Beat to mix thoroughly. Heat an omelet pan and drop in the butter, swirling it so that it coats the bottom and sides. When the butter stops foaming, add the bell pepper and ham, and cook for 1-2 minutes; then add the tomatoes.

Pour in the eggs and, as they begin to cook, push the cooked portion with the flat of a fork to let the uncooked mixture run underneath, so that it begins to cook. Continue to lift the eggs and shake the pan to prevent the omelet from sticking.

When the egg on top is still slightly creamy, fold one-third of the omelet to the center, and tip it out of the pan onto a warmed plate, folded side down. Serve immediately.

EGGS BAKED IN TARRAGON CREAM

There are two types of tarragon, French and Russian, and the French definitely has the finer flavor. It is reminiscent of aniseed, a delicious seasoning for light dishes, especially poultry and eggs. Use freshly laid, free-range eggs for this dish if possible.

Serves 4

INGREDIENTS
Knob of butter
4 large fresh eggs
1 tbsp freshly chopped French
  tarragon
Salt and freshly ground black
  pepper
4 tablespoons heavy cream

Preheat the oven to 350°F. Butter 4 ovenproof ramekins, and break an egg into each one. Stir the chopped tarragon, salt and pepper into the cream, and mix well; then spoon 1 tablespoon of the cream mixture over each egg.

Place the ramekins on a baking sheet, and cook in the oven until set, in about 6-8 minutes. Serve hot.

GOUGÈRE AU JAMBON

A gougère is a large, savoury choux pastry, usually served sliced. Such dishes originated in the Burgundy area, but regional variations are now popular throughout France. A gougère makes an unusual appetizer or an excellent lunch dish.

Serves 4-6

INGREDIENTS
Choux Paste
⅔ cup water
¼ cup butter or margarine
½ cup all-purpose flour, sifted
Salt, freshly ground black pepper
  and dry mustard
2 eggs, beaten
½ cup finely diced cheese

Ham Salpicon
1 tablespoon butter or margarine
2 tablespoons all-purpose flour
⅔ cup stock
Salt and freshly ground black
  pepper
2 teaspoons freshly chopped
  herbs
⅔ cup sliced mushrooms
4 ounces cooked ham, cut into
  thin strips
1 tablespoon grated cheese
1 tablespoon dry bread crumbs

Preheat the oven to 400°F. Prepare the choux pastry. Put the water into a small saucepan; then cut the butter into small pieces, and add it to the water. Bring slowly to a boil, making sure that the butter is completely melted before the water reaches a rapid boil. Increase the heat, and let the mixture boil rapidly for 30 seconds. Sift the flour with a pinch of salt onto a sheet of paper. Take the pan off the heat, and tip all the flour in at once. Stir quickly and vigorously until the mixture comes away from the sides of the pan. Let cool slightly.

Melt the butter for the salpicon in a small saucepan, and add the flour. Cook for 1-2 minutes until browned to a pale straw color. Gradually whisk in the stock, and add a little salt and pepper and the chopped herbs. Stir in the sliced mushrooms and ham, and set aside.

Add a little salt, pepper and the dry mustard to the choux paste, then gradually add the beaten eggs, beating well between each addition – this may be done by hand, or with an electric mixer. It may not be necessary to add all the egg – the mixture should be smooth and shiny, and hold its shape when ready. Stir in the diced cheese.

Spoon the choux paste into a large ovenproof dish or 4 individual dishes, pushing the mixture slightly up the sides of the dish and leaving a well in the center. The paste may be piped into a large circle on a lightly greased baking sheet. Fill the center with the ham salpicon. Mix together the grated cheese and the bread crumbs, and scatter the mixture over the gougère. Bake for about 30 minutes, or until the paste is puffed and browned. Serve immediately.

CHEESE AIGRETTES

These fried choux buns may be served with a salad garnish as an appetizer, or as a cocktail canapé at a drinks party. They are always popular, so make lots!

Serves 4 as an appetizer

INGREDIENTS

Cheese Choux Paste
⅔ cup water
¼ cup butter, cut into small pieces
½ cup plus 2 tablespoons all-purpose flour, sifted
2 eggs, beaten
½ cup finely diced or grated Gruyère or Cheddar cheese
Salt and freshly ground black pepper
Pinch of dry mustard
Parmesan cheese (optional)
Oil for deep-frying

Bring the water and the butter slowly to a boil in a heavy-bottomed saucepan – make sure that the butter has melted before the water boils. Heat until boiling rapidly; then move the pan to one side, and shoot in the sifted flour all at once. Beat vigorously until smooth – the mixture will form a ball and leave the sides of the pan. Let cool slightly, then beat in the eggs, one at a time, until the choux paste is smooth and glossy. Add the cheese, and season to taste with salt, pepper and mustard. This paste can be prepared a few hours ahead, and kept in the refrigerator, covered with a damp cloth.

Heat the oil in a deep-frying kettle until moderately hot, about 350°F. Carefully drop in a teaspoonful of mixture at a time – do not fry too many aigrettes at once as they need space to swell during cooking. Cook the aigrettes for 5-6 minutes, until puffed and golden-brown. Remove from the kettle with a draining spoon, and drain on paper towels; then dredge lightly with grated Parmesan cheese. Repeat the frying process until all the mixture has been used. Serve hot.

CROQUE MONSIEUR

This is a simple fried sandwich, an ideal appetizer or savory snack. Cut small, these make delicious cocktail party canapés; left in larger pieces, they make an excellent light lunch dish.

Serves 4

INGREDIENTS
8 medium slices white bread
⅓ cup butter
4 slices lean ham
1 cup grated Gruyère cheese
Oil for frying

Butter the bread, and lay the ham and cheese on 4 of the slices. Cover with the remaining bread, and press the slices firmly together. Cut off the crusts, and cut each sandwich into 3 fingers. Fry in hot oil until golden – the sandwiches may be deep- or shallow-fried. Drain on paper towels and serve at once.

CHEESE PUFFS

These puffs are similar to the classic Cheese Aigrettes, except they are baked rather than fried. The puffs also have a cheese filling. Serve as a cocktail party canapé.

Makes about 24

INGREDIENTS
Choux Paste
1 cup all-purpose flour
Pinch of salt
⅓ cup butter or margarine, cut into small pieces
1 cup water
3 medium eggs, lightly beaten

Filling
Generous ½ cup grated Gruyère cheese
Generous ½ cup grated Emmenthal cheese
1 egg, lightly beaten
2 teaspoons Kirsch

1 egg yolk, beaten, for glazing

Preheat the oven to 425°F. Lightly grease two baking sheets.

Sift together the flour and salt onto a sheet of baking parchment. Melt the butter in the water, bringing it slowly to a boil. Remove the pan from the heat when a rolling boil is achieved, and shoot in the flour.

Beat vigorously until smooth – the mixture will form a ball and come away from the sides of the pan. Let cool slightly, then gradually beat in the eggs to give a smooth shiny dough of piping consistency – do not add all the beaten egg if it is not required.

Pipe the paste into walnut-size balls on the prepared baking sheets, or use 2 teaspoons to make small mounds of the mixture. Bake for 10-15 minutes, until firm on the outside. Remove from the oven, and reduce the temperature to 400°F.

To make the filling, beat the grated cheeses together, add the egg and Kirsch. Place the mixture in a piping bag fitted with a ¼-inch tip. Pipe a little of the mixture into each bun, through the base or the side, and brush each one with a little egg yolk.

Return the cheese puffs to the oven for an additional 5 minutes. Serve warm, straight from the oven.

CAMEMBERT FRITTERS

Deep-fried Camembert is one of my favorite appetizers, although I always have a twinge of guilt when I indulge because of my waistline! This is an interesting variation on the theme. Serve the fritters freshly cooked with a light salad garnish and a little redcurrant or blackberry jelly.

Serves 4-5

INGREDIENTS
Béchamel Sauce
1¼ cups milk
1 small onion
1 bay leaf
10 black peppercorns
¼ cup butter
½ cup flour

8 ounces Camembert cheese
3 egg yolks
1 teaspoon Dijon mustard
Salt and freshly ground black
  pepper
Oil for deep-frying
Seasoned flour
2 eggs, beaten
1½-2 cups fresh white bread
  crumbs

Put the milk, onion, bay leaf and peppercorns into a medium saucepan, and bring slowly to a boil. Remove the pan from the heat, cover with a lid, and let infuse for 30 minutes. Strain the milk into a jug.

Melt the butter in a saucepan. Add the flour, and stir continuously for 1 minute over a low heat. Gradually add the strained milk, and heat until the sauce is boiling, thickened and smooth. Cut the rind away from the cheese and discard it; then chop the remaining cheese into small pieces, and add to the béchamel sauce, together with the egg yolks. Simmer gently for 2-3 minutes, stirring constantly, until the cheese has melted. Remove the pan from the heat, and add the mustard and seasonings. Pour into a shallow cake pan or jelly roll pan, to a depth of ½-inch, and let cool. The fritter mixture may be made a day ahead, and kept in the refrigerator, or frozen until needed.

Using a small cooky cutter about 1½ inches in diameter, cut out rounds of the cheese mixture. Dip the rounds in the seasoned flour, then in the beaten egg, and finally coat with the bread crumbs, pressing them lightly into the surface of the fritters with your fingers.

Heat the oil in a deep-frying kettle or large saucepan with a draining basket to 350°F, and fry the fritters, a few at a time, until golden – this will take 1½-2 minutes. Remove the fritters from the oil with a draining spoon, drain on paper towels,and keep them warm on a serving dish while frying the rest of the fritters.

Serve garnished with a little parsley or watercress, and with a cranberry or redcurrant sauce.

TAPENADE

This recipe is popular throughout France, but originates in the south, in Provence, where many of the ingredients are in almost daily use. It may be served as a dip, spread onto bread, or stirred into savory casseroles or rice dishes at the end of the cooking period. Some people add tuna to their tapenade, but this, although delicious, is not traditional.

Serves 4

INGREDIENTS
2-ounce can anchovy fillets in
  olive oil
10 black olives, pitted
⅔ cup olive oil
2 tablespoons brandy
1 teaspoon lemon juice
2 tablespoons capers
1 tablespoon Dijon mustard
1 teaspoon fresh thyme
Freshly ground black pepper

Purée all the ingredients together in a blender or food processor until smooth, or pound to a smooth paste in a pestle and mortar, gradually adding the olive oil. Season to taste with freshly ground black pepper.

ANCHOÏADE

This strongly savory anchovy paste is fantastic when spread on small crisp toasts and served as a cocktail canapé, garnished with hard-cooked egg and mock caviar. It may also be served as an appetizer with the toasts presented on a bed of lettuce.

Serves 6

INGREDIENTS
15 salted anchovy fillets
2 cloves garlic
½ cup olive oil; a fruity, green extra virgin oil is best
Few drops lemon juice
Freshly ground black pepper to taste
12 small slices of bread, toasted

To serve as an appetizer
1 lettuce, washed and torn into small pieces
4 tablespoons vinaigrette dressing (see recipe)

If serving the anchoïade as an appetizer, toss the prepared lettuce in the vinaigrette. Rinse the anchovy fillets under cold running water to remove the excess salt, then pat them dry on paper towels.

Pound the garlic with a pestle and mortar until it is smooth; then add the anchovies, and work them into the garlic. Beat in the oil, a little at a time, until a smooth paste is formed, and season to taste with lemon juice and pepper.

Spread the mixture onto the slices of toast. Serve on a bed of the tossed lettuce, if wished.

FISH & SHELLFISH

France has three main coasts yielding a fine selection of fish and shellfish. The Mediterranean, the Atlantic Ocean and the English Channel (or should I say, La Manche?) give rise to famous dishes in the south, the west and the north of France. The many rivers throughout the country are home to freshwater fish, and the French also add variety by the use of salt cod. It is an understatement to say that the French are fond of fish, and a banality to comment that they have some fine recipes for it. In my opinion they are the finest fish cooks in the world, and the huge selection of vegetables and other ingredients available to cook with the fish gives a versatility of cuisine that is second to none.

Just the Weather for Fishing

One thing that really makes French fish cookery stand out in my mind is that the people understand the effect that the weather can have on the availability of fish. This was illustrated to me when staying with a family in Normandy. Asked what I would like to eat on Sunday, I had indicated a preference for seafood, and our host had planned to prepare *Fruits de Mer* for us. However, the weather was stormy, and had not improved by the Sunday morning. Michel insisted on totally re-planning the lunch menu – if he couldn't obtain fresh fish, he certainly was not to be content with frozen. Frozen fish is convenient, but not the same as a really fresh catch. Fish is rather like herbs – if one variety is not available, use another fresh one rather than a preserved version of the first choice.

A Celebration of Flavor

Although the French are very much more inventive than, say, the average American in their approach to fish cookery (yes, there is more to it than batter and French fries!) it is interesting to note that on the majority of occasions even the greatest of chefs will choose to cook fish simply, barbecuing or broiling it and serving an accompanying sauce, baking it whole, or making one of the great fish soups such as *Bouillabaisse*. Perhaps a chef in an expensive city restaurant might consider stuffing a fish with a mousse and serving it in a lobster sauce, but the regional chefs and home cooks would celebrate the freshness and flavor of the catch by simple preparation and light but inspired seasoning.

Experiment with Different Fish

Rouget, or red mullet, is a fish that has long been popular in France. If unavailable, it can be substituted by red snapper. Choose larger fish to get as much meat to bone as possible, and scale the fish thoroughly before cooking. Red mullet has a very different flavor to white fish, and even to some of the oily fish such as mackerel – it actually has a flavor distinctly reminiscent of game! This makes it an excellent fish to barbecue, and it is also one of the few fish that can withstand really robust seasoning with olives, strong herbs and garlic. Red Mullet Niçoise, for example, is an unusual and delicious fish recipe that really packs a punch!

I first discovered John Dory (or St Peter's Fish) and monkfish when I was *sous-chef d'un jour* for Roger Vergé, *Chef Patron* of Le Moulin de Mougins near Cannes. I had never heard of these fish, and yet now, almost two decades later, they are enjoying virtually the same popularity in England as they have had in France for many years. I have never been lucky enough to purchase monkfish other than from the tail, and this meat is covered with a thick transparent membrane that must be removed before cooking as it will toughen dramatically. The meat itself can be filleted away from the bone, and will keep its shape well during cooking.

Whatever your favorite fish, the French will have a dish for it, the perfect recipe blending the best ingredients. We should all learn to appreciate fish as much as they do – in that way we would keep many of our traditional recipes alive, certainly those for river fish and the less popular saltwater varieties.

COD WITH LEEKS

Large slices of cod are required for this dish. Keep the skin on the fish for an attractive presentation. This dish can be prepared with other types of fish if cod is not available.

Serves 4

INGREDIENTS

2 thick pieces of cod, about 12 ounces each

Salt and and freshly ground black pepper

2 pounds leeks, well rinsed and drained

2 cups light cream

1 tablespoon freshly chopped chives

Cut each piece of cod into two, removing any bones. Sprinkle with salt and pepper, and keep in a cool place. Cut the leeks into very thin slices, and put them into a skillet. Add the cream. Cook over a low heat for 10 minutes, covered. Add the fish to the leeks, and continue cooking for 10 minutes. Serve the leek and cream base on a warmed plate with the cod fillets placed on top and the chives sprinkled over.

BOW TIE SOLE FILLETS IN OYSTER SAUCE

With the rich flavor of oyster sauce, this is an imaginative way of serving sole – an ideal dinner party dish. Use the best quality oysters on the market, they make all the difference to this dish. They should be firm with not too much juice in the shell. The oysters should be cooked for a maximum of 2 minutes; otherwise they will shrink.

Serves 6

INGREDIENTS
3 large sole fillets
2½ cups finely sliced mushrooms
2 tomatoes, diced
2 cups fish stock
3 tablespoons heavy cream
12 oysters, shells removed
Salt and freshly ground black
   pepper

Cut the sole fillets lengthwise into four strips, and tie each piece into a knot; this makes the "bow tie." In a large skillet, cook the mushrooms and half of the tomatoes in the stock for 5 minutes. Carefully lower the "bow ties" into the stock, and cook over a low heat for an additional 5 minutes or so – cooking time will depend on the thickness of the fillets. Carefully remove the cooked fillets with a draining spoon.

Remove the sauce from the heat, and stir in the cream. Arrange the "bow ties" neatly on a preheated serving dish. Blend the sauce with a hand mixer until smooth. Stir the oysters into the sauce just prior to serving. Allow just enough time to heat the oysters, and pour the sauce immediately over the "bow ties." Sprinkle with the remaining diced tomato, and season. Serve immediately.

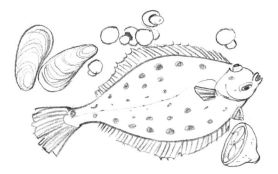

BOUILLABAISSE

Bouillabaisse is the classic fish soup of France, originating from the harbor-side restaurants of Marseilles, one of the busiest fishing ports on the Mediterranean coast. Like so many classic dishes, it has been changed and adapted over the years. This recipe makes a delicious fish soup – but purists would say that the only way to eat Bouillabaisse is in a bistro in Marseilles!

Serves 4

INGREDIENTS

4½ pounds fresh mixed Mediterranean fish and shellfish, such as whiting, mullet, mussels, shrimp, John Dory – fillet the fish and reserve all the bones and trimmings
2 onions, finely chopped
1 sprig fennel
¼ cup olive oil
2 cloves garlic, crushed
1 teaspoon freshly chopped thyme
1 bay leaf
Pinch of saffron
Salt and freshly ground black pepper
4 large tomatoes, skinned and sliced
2 large potatoes, diced

Prepare the fish. Skin the fillets, and cut the flesh into large pieces. Scrub the mussels, and remove any beards. Put the fish bones into a large pan with half the onion and the fennel. Cover with plenty of cold water, and simmer for 15 minutes to make a fish stock. Strain the stock and discard the bones.

Heat the oil in a large pan. Add the remaining onion and the garlic, and cook until soft. Add all the seasonings, the tomatoes and potatoes, then add the stock. Bring to a boil, and simmer for 20 minutes, or until the potato is cooked. Add the prepared fish and shellfish, and cook for an additional 10 minutes. Add extra stock or water to the pan if necessary.

Season the Bouillabaisse to taste. The fish is traditionally served in one bowl with the broth served separately in another. Serve with croûtes of French bread topped with Rouille (see Soupe de Poisson Provençale).

MATELOTE

A "matelot" is actually a boatman! However, "matelote" is a name given to a fish stew. There are many recipes for matelote from all over France, each one varying in its use of local fish and wine.

Serves 4

INGREDIENTS

1 pound brill or lemon sole
1 pound monkfish
1 small wing of skate
8 ounces unshelled cooked
  shrimp
2½ pints mussels
3 onions, finely chopped
⅓ cup butter
2 cups dry cider or white wine
¼ cup all-purpose flour
2 tablespoons freshly chopped
  parsley
Salt and freshly ground black
  pepper
Lemon juice

Fillet and skin the brill or lemon sole, then cut the fillets into large pieces. Cut the monkfish into similar size pieces, and cut the skate into four. shell the shrimp, then scrub the mussels, removing any beards and discarding any mussels with cracked or broken shells.

Soften the onions in half the butter, then add the mussels and 3-4 tablespoons of water. Cover the pan, and shake it over a high heat until all the mussels have opened. Do not overcook the mussels as they will toughen – discard any which remain tightly closed. Strain the cooking liquor into a bowl.

Return the cooking liquor to the pan, and add the cider or wine. Add the fish to the pan, and simmer over a low heat for 5-8 minutes, until the fish is just cooked. Remove the fish to a serving dish, and keep it warm in a low oven. Return the cooking liquor to a boil. Mix the flour with the remaining butter, and whisk it, a little at a time, into the liquid. Let the liquid boil after each addition.

Add the parsley, shrimp, mussels, and lemon juice, and seasoning to taste to the sauce, and cook briefly to reheat the shellfish. Adjust the seasoning, and spoon over the fish in the serving dish. Garnish with a little extra chopped parsley, and serve.

TROUT FILLETS WITH FISH ROE SAUCE

The original presentation of the trout fillets provides another visually appealing dish.

Serves 4

INGREDIENTS
4 trout, filleted
Salt and freshly ground black
  pepper
1¼ cups fish stock
⅔ cup heavy cream
4 tablespoons fish roe, lumpfish,
  keta or salmon trout

Cut the trout fillets in two, crosswise. Place four pieces on a sheet of lightly greased foil, overlapping the long sides and alternating one piece skin-side up, the next with flesh-side up. Sprinkle with salt and pepper, and then close the foil around the fish. Repeat the process with the remaining pieces of trout to make four packages all together. Put the stock into a saucepan over a high heat, and let reduce by half. Stir in the cream, and reduce a little more. Purée the sauce in a blender or food processor, and keep warm over a saucepan of hot water. Steam the fish in their packages for 10-15 minutes, or until cooked through, then remove the foil. Serve on warmed plates with the sauce poured around the fish and the roe sprinkled over.

SKATE WITH BLACK BUTTER

Skate is one of my favorite fish, and this recipe, where it is cooked in black butter, is probably the all-time classic recipe for the fish. The first time that you prepare this you will need a certain amount of courage to actually cook the butter until it browns – don't worry, it will not taste burned; it will taste wonderful!

Serves 4

INGREDIENTS
4 wings of skate
1 slice onion
2 stalks parsley
Pinch of salt
6 black peppercorns

Black Butter
¼ cup butter
1 tablespoon capers
2 tablespoons white wine vinegar
1 tablespoon freshly chopped
  parsley (optional)

Place the skate wings in one layer in a large, deep skillet. Cover the fish completely with water, and add the onion, parsley, salt and peppercorns. Bring slowly to a boil and simmer gently for 10-15 minutes, or until the skate is cooked. Lift the fish out carefully onto a warmed serving dish, and remove the skin and any large pieces of bone. Take care not to break up the fish.

Prepare the butter while the fish is finishing cooking. Put the butter into a small pan, and cook over a high heat until it begins to brown. Add the capers, and immediately remove the butter from the heat. Add the vinegar, which will cause the butter to bubble, and add the parsley. Pour the butter immediately over the fish, and serve.

PROVENÇAL RED MULLET

Red mullet is a meaty, gamy fish – it is sometimes known as the "woodcock of the sea" because it is often served with the liver left inside, the traditional way of serving woodcock. In this recipe the mullet is cooked with tomatoes and herbs, some of the traditional ingredients of Provence.

Serves 4

INGREDIENTS

2 tablespoons olive oil
1 clove garlic, crushed
2 shallots, finely chopped
1 pound ripe tomatoes, skinned, seeded and sliced
2 teaspoons freshly chopped marjoram and parsley, mixed
⅓ cup dry white wine
Salt and freshly ground black pepper
Pinch of saffron
Oil for frying
2 small bulbs fennel, quartered and cored
4 red mullet, about 6 ounces each
Seasoned flour

Heat the olive oil in a deep saucepan, and add the garlic and shallots. Cook for 1-2 minutes until slightly softened, then add the tomatoes, herbs, wine, salt and pepper, and saffron. Simmer, uncovered, for 30 minutes (adding a little water or stock if necessary), then set to one side while preparing the fennel and fish.

Pour about 4 tablespoons oil into a large skillet or sauté pan. Put over a moderate heat, and add the fennel. Cook quickly until the fennel is slightly browned, then lower the heat, and cook for an additional 5-10 minutes to soften the fennel. Remove it from the pan.

Scale the mullet. Remove the gills and clean the fish, leaving the liver. Wash the fish, and dry thoroughly. Trim the fins, and roll the mullet in seasoned flour, shaking off any excess.

Fry the mullet in the fennel-flavored oil until golden-brown, about 5 minutes on each side. Arrange the fish in a warmed serving dish, and surround them with the fennel. Reheat the tomato sauce, and spoon some over the fish. Serve any remaining sauce separately.

TRUITES MEUNIÈRE AUX HERBES

Meunière is a term often applied to the cooking of fish. Tradition has it that a miller would catch fish from the mill stream, and his wife, the meunière, would dredge them in freshly milled flour before cooking. Well, it's a good little story – and an excellent way of cooking fish.

Serves 4

INGREDIENTS
4 even-size trout, cleaned and
  trimmed
Flour
Salt and freshly ground black
  pepper
½ cup butter
Juice of 1 lemon
2 tablespoons freshly chopped
  herbs such as parsley, chervil,
  tarragon, thyme or marjoram
Lemon wedges to garnish

Trim the trout tails to make them more pointed, then rinse the fish well. Dredge the trout with flour, and shake off any excess, then season with salt and pepper. Heat half the butter in a very large sauté pan. When foaming, add the trout. It may be necessary to cook the fish in two batches to avoid overcrowding the pan. Cook over a fairly high heat on both sides to brown evenly. Depending on size, the trout should take 5-8 minutes on each side to cook. The dorsal fin will pull out easily when the trout are ready. Remove the fish to a serving dish, and keep them warm.

Wipe out the pan, and add the remaining butter. Cook over a medium heat until the butter is beginning to brown, then add the lemon juice and herbs. The butter will bubble up and sizzle when the lemon juice is added. Pour the butter over the fish immediately, and serve with wedges of lemon.

PROVENÇAL FISH STEW

This is a hearty stew of shellfish, tomatoes, garlic and red wine – a dish for fish lovers everywhere. Choose a fairly robust red wine, a Côtes du Rhône would be my choice. Serve the stew with crusty bread for mopping up the delicious juices.

Serves 4

INGREDIENTS

1 medium onion, finely chopped
2 cloves garlic, crushed
3 tablespoons olive oil
1½ pounds tomatoes, skinned, seeded and chopped
2½ cups dry red wine
2 tablespoons tomato paste
Salt and freshly ground black pepper
2½ pints fresh mussels in their shells, scrubbed and debearded
8 large, cooked jumbo shrimp
1 cup cooked, shelled shrimp
4 crab claws, shelled but with the claw tips left intact

Fry the onion and garlic together over a low heat in the olive oil, until soft but not brown. Add the tomatoes, and fry until they are beginning to soften; then stir in the red wine and tomato paste. Season to taste. Bring the mixture to a boil, cover and simmer for about 15 minutes. Add the mussels to the pan, cover and steam for about 5 minutes, shaking the pan frequently, until the mussel shells have opened. Discard any mussels that do not open.

Stir in the remaining ingredients, and cook, uncovered, for 3-5 minutes, or until the shrimp and crab claws are thoroughly heated. Season to taste, and serve.

NIÇOIS RED MULLET

Red mullet is one of the few fish that is able to cope with strong flavorings, such as olives, bell peppers, garlic and mustard. This is a well-flavored, colorful salad, redolent of Mediterranean sunshine!

Serves 4

INGREDIENTS
2 tablespoons red wine vinegar
8 tablespoons olive oil
4 teaspoons French mustard
Handful of freshly chopped
  mixed herbs
1 shallot, finely chopped
1 clove garlic, crushed
Salt and freshly ground black
  pepper
4 ounces button mushrooms,
  quartered
4 red mullet, scaled and cleaned
Seasoned flour
Lemon juice
1 pound tomatoes, quartered and
  cores removed
1 green bell pepper, seeded and
  sliced
¾ cup pitted black olives, halved
2 hard-cooked eggs, quartered
2-ounce can anchovy fillets

Shake together the vinegar, 4 tablespoons of the oil, the mustard, herbs, shallot, garlic, and salt and pepper into a screw-topped jar. Put the mushrooms into a bowl and add the vinaigrette. Stir to coat the mushrooms evenly, then chill them for about an hour.

Toss the mullet in the seasoned flour. Heat the remaining oil in a skillet, and fry the fish on both sides for about 5 minutes on each side, taking care not to break the fish when turning them. Sprinkle lightly with lemon juice and salt and pepper, then leave until cold.

When ready to serve, add the tomatoes, bell pepper, olives and eggs to the mushrooms. Stir together gently, to coat all the salad ingredients with the marinade. Pile the salad onto a serving dish, and arrange the red mullet on top. Garnish with the drained anchovy fillets, and serve.

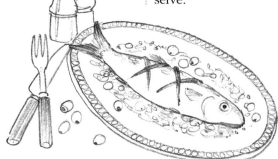

BROILED RED MULLET WITH TARRAGON

Red mullet is widely used in France and, because of its attractive appearance, it is now becoming more and more popular in other countries. It has a much stronger flavor than many other fish – here that flavor is balanced by seasoning the fish with tarragon.

Serves 4

INGREDIENTS

4 large or 8 small red mullet, gutted, scaled, washed and dried
Salt and freshly ground black pepper
4 or 8 sprigs of fresh tarragon
4 tablespoons vegetable oil
2 tablespoons tarragon vinegar
1 egg
1 teaspoon Dijon mustard
½ cup sunflower oil
1 tablespoon wine vinegar
1 teaspoon brandy
1 tablespoon freshly chopped tarragon
1 tablespoon freshly chopped parsley
1 tablespoon heavy cream

Rub the inside of each mullet with a teaspoonful of salt, scrubbing hard to remove any discolored membranes inside. Rinse thoroughly, then place a sprig of fresh tarragon inside each fish. Using a sharp knife, cut 2 diagonal slits on the side of each fish – this helps to speed even cooking.

Mix the vegetable oil, tarragon vinegar and a little salt and pepper together in a small bowl. Arrange the fish in a shallow dish, and pour the vinegar marinade over, brushing some of the mixture into the cuts on the sides of the fish. Chill for 30 minutes.

Put the egg into a blender or food processor with the mustard and a little salt and pepper. Blend for 2-3 seconds to mix, then, with the machine running, add the oil through the feed-tube in a thin, steady stream. Continue blending the dressing until it is thick and creamy. Add the wine vinegar, brandy and herbs, and process for a further 30 seconds to mix well. Lightly whip the cream with a small whisk until it thickens. Fold the cream carefully into the oil and vinegar dressing. Pour into a serving dish, and chill until ready to use.

Arrange the fish on a broiler pan rack and cook under a preheated broiler for 5-8 minutes on each side, depending on the size of the fish. Baste frequently with the marinade during cooking. Serve with a little of the sauce and some sprigs of fresh tarragon.

RED MULLET WITH HERBS "EN PAPILLOTE"

Cooking "en papillote" means cooking in a package, with the food wrapped up to keep it moist in its juices. Baking parchment is the most traditional wrapping, although foil can also be used. Parchment looks good, and the food is often presented at the table still wrapped – foil is not so attractive, and should be removed before serving.

Serves 4

INGREDIENTS
Oil
4 red mullet, gutted and trimmed
¼ cup butter
3 shallots, finely chopped
4 tablespoons freshly chopped herbs such as chervil, tarragon, marjoram, basil and parsley
Salt and freshly ground black pepper
4 tablespoons dry white wine
Lemon wedges or slices for garnish

Preheat the oven to 350°F. Cut 4 rounds of baking parchment or foil large enough to enclose the fish. Brush the rounds with oil, and place a fish on the lower half of each. Melt the butter in a small pan. Add the shallots, and cook until lightly browned, then add the herbs, and salt and pepper. Pour 1 tablespoon of wine over each fish, then spoon the butter mixture over. Fold the parchment or foil over the mullet, and seal the ends. Place the papillotes in a roasting pan or on a baking sheet with a lip around the edge, in case the packages leak.

Cook the red mullet in the oven for about 20-25 minutes; the cooking time will vary according to the size of the fish. Place the packages on individual serving plates, and let each person open their own. Serve with lemon wedges.

SWORDFISH STEAKS WITH GREEN PEPPERCORNS AND GARLIC SAUCE

Swordfish is a very meaty fish, slightly pink in color when raw but white when cooked. It is inclined to dryness so the best way to prepare swordfish is by marinating it. In this recipe the steaks are broiled – they also barbecue well. The garlic sauce served with the swordfish is an aïoli, a rich garlic mayonnaise.

Serves 4

INGREDIENTS
2 tablespoons green peppercorns
6 tablespoons lemon juice
4 tablespoons olive oil
Freshly ground sea salt
4 swordfish steaks

Aïoli
1 egg
1 clove garlic, roughly chopped
⅔ cup oil
2 teaspoons freshly chopped oregano
Freshly ground black pepper

Crush the green peppercorns lightly using a pestle and mortar, then mix them with the lemon juice, olive oil and salt. Place the swordfish steaks in a shallow ovenproof dish, and pour the lemon and oil mixture over the fish, coating each steak.

Chill for 6-8 hours or overnight, turning occasionally, until the fish becomes opaque.

To make the aïoli, combine the egg and garlic together in a blender or food processor. With the motor running, gradually add the oil through the feed-tube in a thin, steady stream. Continue to blend until the sauce is thick.

Preheat the broiler until very hot, and arrange the swordfish in the broiler pan. Sprinkle the chopped oregano over the swordfish steaks, and season well. Cook for 15 minutes, turning frequently and basting with the lemon and pepper marinade.

Arrange the cooked swordfish steaks on a warmed serving dish, and spoon the aïoli over to serve.

CRISPY GRIDDLED MACKEREL

Mackerel is a rich, flavorsome fish – a common catch along the north coast of France. It benefits from the simplest of cooking – pan-frying or cooking on a hot griddle.

Serves 4-8

INGREDIENTS

8 medium fresh mackerel, gutted, washed and wiped dry
1 cup all-purpose
⅔ cup oil
Salt

To Serve

2 lemons, cut into quarters
2 tablespoons freshly chopped parsley

Make sure the mackerel are really dry: use paper towels to soak up every last drop of water. Preheat a griddle or skillet until very hot. Roll each fish in the flour, shaking off any excess; then dip the floured fish into the oil, and sprinkle with the salt. Place them on the griddle or in the skillet and cook until crisp – this takes about 15 minutes if the mackerel are of average thickness. Turn the fish once during cooking – do not attempt this before the mackerel are ready and will not stick to the surface, otherwise they will stick and the presentation will be spoiled. Sprinkle with salt and chopped parsley before serving.

GOUJONS OF SOLE

The term "goujon" is applied to small pieces of fish, coated in bread crumbs and fried. Sole is the fish most frequently served in this way. The curry and tomato sauces give an excellent variety of dips for serving with the sole.

Serves 4

INGREDIENTS
2 lemon soles, filleted and
  skinned
Seasoned flour
1 egg, lightly beaten
2 teaspoons olive oil
Dry bread crumbs
Oil for deep-frying
Pinch of salt
Lemon wedges

Tartare Sauce
2 tablespoons mayonnaise
1 tablespoon heavy cream
2 teaspoons freshly chopped
  parsley
2 teaspoons chopped gherkins
2 teaspoons chopped capers
1 teaspoon chopped onion

Curry Sauce
2 tablespoons mayonnaise
1 tablespoon heavy cream
1 teaspoon curry paste
1½ teaspoons mango chutney

Tomato Herb Sauce
2 tablespoons mayonnaise
1 tablespoon heavy cream
1 teaspoon freshly chopped
  parsley
1 teaspoon freshly chopped
  chives
1 teaspoon tomato paste
Lemon juice

Cut the sole fillets on the diagonal into pieces about ½ inch thick and 2½-3 inches long. Coat the fish thoroughly in seasoned flour, then shake to remove any excess. Beat the egg lightly with the olive oil.

Prepare the various sauces simply by combining the ingredients together. Put into small serving dishes, and set aside until the sole is cooked.

Heat some oil in a deep-frying kettle to 375°F. Dip the floured fish in the beaten egg, then coat the fish pieces in the bread crumbs. Lower the goujons into the oil in a wire basket, and cook until crisp and golden in 2-3 minutes. Cook the sole in two or three batches to prevent the pieces sticking together during cooking.

Drain the cooked fish on paper towels. Sprinkle lightly with salt, and pile into a hot serving dish. Continue frying until all the sole is cooked; then serve, garnished with parsley and lemon wedges, with the sauces handed separately for dipping.

TRUITE EN PAPILLOTE

Cooking "en papillote" is a simple but effective way of preparing fish, keeping it moist during cooking and giving an attractive style of presentation. Foil may be used in place of baking parchment, but I don't think that it is so attractive for serving, so I would recommend that you unwrap the fish in the kitchen if you do use foil.

Serves 4

INGREDIENTS
4 small trout, cleaned, each about 8 ounces in weight
Salt and freshly ground black pepper
Sprigs of rosemary
2–3 shallots
½ cup butter
Lemon juice
1 cup slivered almonds
Lemon slices to garnish

Preheat the oven to 350°F. Trim the fins of the trout, and lightly season the cavities, placing a small sprig of rosemary in each, and making two or three slits in each side of each fish to speed cooking. Finely chop the shallots. Melt half the butter.

Cut four large rounds of baking parchment. Brush them with the butter, and place a fish on each. Scatter the trout with the shallots, a little salt and pepper and some lemon juice, then pour the melted butter over the fish. Fold the parchment up over the trout, and seal well. Place the packages on a baking sheet and bake for 10-15 minutes.

Brown the almonds in the remaining butter, adding salt, pepper and a good squeeze of lemon juice. Add a little freshly chopped rosemary to the almonds just before serving.

Serve each trout in its package, slightly opened, and with a little of the hot butter and almonds spooned over the fish. Garnish with lemon slices.

SEA BREAM WITH PEPPERCORN SAUCE

Filleting fish is easy to do at home, provided you have a sharp knife. A good fish vendor will, however, be happy to fillet the fish for you. I leave the skin on the fillets when broiling them, as it makes the fish easier to turn, with less risk of it breaking up.

Serves 6

INGREDIENTS

2 large sea bream, filleted
1 tablespoon olive oil
10 green peppercorns
1 tablespoon Cognac
2 shallots, skinned and finely chopped
1 tomato, seeded and chopped
⅓ cup of Noilly Pratt vermouth
⅔ cup white wine
1 tablespoon sugar
1 cup heavy cream
Salt

Fillet the bream, then set them to one side. Heat the olive oil in a skillet, and sauté the peppercorns for about 1 minute. Pour off the oil. Add the Cognac, and cook until almost evaporated. Add the shallots, tomato, vermouth, white wine and sugar. Stir well and let the mixture thicken until quite syrupy. This may take quite a while if the tomato is very juicy. While the sauce is thickening, cook the fish fillets under a hot broiler – this will take 4-5 minutes. Stir the cream into the sauce over a very low heat, insuring that the sauce does not boil. Season with salt. Purée the sauce until smooth in a blender or food processor, and serve poured over the hot fish.

SOLE IN RED WINE
SOLE AU VIN ROUGE

Sole is most often cooked in a white wine sauce, and served with white grapes, but red wine makes a surprisingly delicious change. Use a light red wine – a Bordeaux would work well.

Serves 4

INGREDIENTS
2 whole lemon sole, filleted
⅔ cup red wine
5 tablespoons water
1 slice onion
3-4 peppercorns
1 bay leaf
1 small bunch black grapes
1 tablespoon butter
2 tablespoons all-purpose flour
⅔ cup heavy cream
Salt and freshly ground black
    pepper

Preheat the oven to 325°F. Skin the fish fillets, then fold the thin ends of the fillets under to make neat packages of uniform thickness. Place in an ovenproof dish, and pour the wine and water over the fillets. Add the onion, peppercorns, bay leaf and a pinch of salt, then cover the dish with foil. Bake for about 10 minutes.

Wash the grapes and remove the seeds – leave the grapes whole unless they are very large, in which case they should be cut in half.

Remove the sole from the baking dish, cover and keep warm. Strain and reserve the cooking liquor. Melt the butter in a small pan until foaming; then remove the pan from the heat, and stir in the flour. Return to the heat, and cook for 2-3 minutes, stirring continuously, until lightly browned. Gradually whisk in the fish liquor, and heat, stirring continuously, until the sauce boils and thickens. Add the cream, and boil again; then season to taste. Add most of the grapes, and heat slowly.

Arrange the fillets of sole in a serving dish, then spoon the sauce over. Garnish with the remaining grapes before serving.

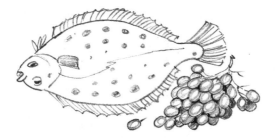

CREAMED SALT COD
BRANDADE DE MORUE

Although salt cod is used throughout France, most of it comes from Brittany or from the Breton fisherman who bring it from Iceland. It was a valuable winter food in years gone by, before refrigeration. Poach the cod slowly, or it may become stringy. Serve with bread or garlic bread and a tomato garnish.

Serves 6

INGREDIENTS
2¼ pounds salt cod
2 cups olive oil
1¼ cups heavy cream
Freshly ground black pepper

Soak the cod for one day in cold water, changing the water frequently to remove the excess salt. Poach the fish in a pan of water for 7 minutes, then drain well. Remove all the bones and the skin, and flake the fish very finely.

In a large saucepan, heat about one quarter of the oil slowly, and add the fish, stirring and mixing well until a fine paste is achieved. Remove from the heat, and, using a spatula, briskly work in the remaining oil and the cream, adding them alternately, little by little. Season well with pepper.

GRIDDLED TUNA STEAKS

Fresh tuna is widely available in supermarkets and fishmarkets. It can be dry if overcooked, and is really at its best when cooked rare, still slightly pink and moist in the center.

Serves 6

INGREDIENTS
6 fresh tuna steaks
4 tablespoons olive oil
2 tablespoons freshly chopped
  mixed herbs

Dressing
1 tomato
1 tablespoon vinegar
2 tablespoons olive oil
1 tablespoon freshly chopped
  herbs
Salt and freshly ground black
  pepper

Remove the bones from the tuna. Shape the fish into rounds and secure around the edges with kitchen string. Place on a shallow plate, and coat with the olive oil, then sprinkle with the herbs. Chill for at least 3 hours.

Preheat a griddle, skillet or barbecue until very hot, and cook the fish until crispy on the outside and just slightly pink in the center – this will take 8-10 minutes. Skin the tomato, and chop it into small dice. Make a vinaigrette by mixing together the vinegar, oil and herbs. Season well with salt and pepper. Stir in the diced tomato, and serve with the fish.

ROLLED SOLE FILLETS

This is the classic way to prepare fillets of sole, although the stuffing may vary according to season and personal choice. The rich, creamy sauce helps to complete a classic dish.

Serves 6

INGREDIENTS

6 medium sole fillets, halved
  lengthwise
2 tablespoons freshly chopped
  herbs, such as parsley, chives
  and basil
2½ cups fish stock
8 ounces chopped mushrooms
1 clove garlic, chopped
1¼ cups heavy cream
Salt and freshly ground black
  pepper

Beat the sole fillets until flat. Place them between 2 sheets of waxed paper or plastic wrap, and flatten with light strokes of a rolling pin. Sprinkle the fresh herbs over the fish. Roll up the fillets, and secure with wooden toothpicks.

Boil the stock in a saucepan over a high heat and let it reduce by half. Add the mushrooms and garlic, and cook for 8 minutes. Remove from the heat. Beat in the cream, and add a little salt and pepper. Remove the mushrooms with a draining spoon and set them aside. Let the stock cool slightly, then purée in a blender or food processor.

Meanwhile, steam the fish rolls until cooked – this will take about 8 minutes. Return the mushrooms to the sauce, and reheat, but do not let the sauce boil. Serve the sole on a warmed serving dish with the sauce poured over.

BROILED TROUT

This is a very easy recipe for cooking trout, and it follows the French philosophy of cooking prime ingredients in a very simple way to celebrate the flavor of the food. Use the roe from the trout, if possible, or soft herring roe, for garnish. Fry the roe, or heat through as necessary. The trout will take 15-20 minutes to cook, depending on size.

Serves 6

Ingredients
6 river trout, cleaned
2 tablespoons olive oil
Salt and freshly ground black pepper
Juice of 1 lemon
4 ounces fresh fish roe

Begin by preparing the trout. Cut off the fins. Wash well under running water, and dry them on paper towels. If using a broiler, set it to high, or heat a flat griddle or skillet. Dip the trout in the olive oil, and sprinkle them with salt and pepper. Cook the fish until crispy on the outside and just tender on the inside – turn once, halfway through cooking. Pour a little lemon juice over each fish, and serve hot with a spoonful of fish roe, if wished.

QUENELLES DE BROCHET
AU BEURRE BLANC

Quenelles are a classic dish – lightly poached mousses of pike served with a buttery sauce and vegetable garnish. They require careful preparation but are well worth the effort.

Serves 4

INGREDIENTS
Quenelles
1 pound pike (or other white fish)
2 cups white bread crumbs
4 tablespoons milk
⅓ cup butter
2 eggs
Salt and white pepper
Nutmeg
Cayenne pepper

Beurre Blanc Sauce
1 small onion, finely chopped
1 tablespoon white wine vinegar

3 tablespoons dry white wine
½ cup unsalted butter, cut into small pieces
Salt
2 tablespoons lemon juice
1 teaspoon freshly chopped chives

Vegetable Garnish
1 carrot, peeled
1 stalk celery, trimmed
1 medium zucchini, trimmed
1 leek, trimmed, with some green attached

First prepare the quenelle mixture. Skin and bone the fish, and cut it into small pieces. Soak the bread crumbs in the milk for a few minutes, then drain away most of the liquid. Put the bread crumbs and fish in a food processor. Melt the butter, then pour it into the fish mixture with the machine running. Process to a smooth purée, then add the eggs and seasonings. Chill the quenelle mixture for at least 1 hour.

Prepare the vegetable garnish. Cut all the vegetables into 2-inch lengths, then cut these into thin julienne strips. Bring a large saucepan of salted water to a boil; add the carrots, and cook for 3 minutes. Add the celery, and cook for an additional 5 minutes. Finally, add the zucchini and leek, and cook for an additional 3 minutes.

While the vegetables are cooking, bring a sauté pan of lightly salted water to a boil. Using two dessert spoons, shape the chilled fish mixture into small oval shapes. Poach the quenelles in the simmering water for 6 minutes, turning them over once during cooking. Remove the quenelles from the pan with a draining spoon; drain and place in a covered dish in a cool oven to keep warm.

To prepare the sauce, put the onion into a small pan with the vinegar and wine. Boil until reduced by half; then remove the pan from the heat; and let cool slightly. Add a few pieces of butter, whisking well to give a smooth creamy sauce. Return the pan to the heat, gradually adding the remaining butter and whisking all the time. Season the sauce, and add the lemon juice then press the sauce through a fine strainer. Adjust the seasoning, then add the drained vegetable garnish and the freshly chopped chives.

Serve the quenelles with the beurre blanc sauce poured over.

MACKEREL WITH PEPPERCORNS

Smoked fish is very popular in France, and so are vinaigrette dressings. Combine the two, and you have a most delicious but simple salad. The strong flavor of the mackerel is complemented by a well-flavored dressing.

Serves 6

INGREDIENTS
1 tablespoon wine vinegar
Salt and freshly ground black
 pepper
3 tablespoons olive oil
3 shallots, finely chopped
3 whole smoked mackerel with
 peppercorns, halved, or 6
 smoked mackerel fillets
2 lollorosso lettuces, washed and
 dried
2 tomatoes, skinned, seeded and
 diced
2 sprigs fresh fennel, snipped

Make the vinaigrette by beating together the vinegar, salt and pepper, oil and shallots. Cut the mackerel into fairly thick slices. Place the prepared lettuce on a serving plate. Add the slices of mackerel, and pour the vinaigrette dressing over. Garnish with the diced tomato and the snipped fennel sprigs, and serve immediately.

SCALLOPS WITH FRESH BASIL

This dish is so incredibly simple and so utterly luxurious! It is also quick. Do not attempt to prepare the scallops or the endive ahead as they will spoil – this has to be prepared at the last moment.

Serves 4-6

INGREDIENTS
8 heads endive
½ cup butter
Salt and white pepper
2 cloves garlic, finely chopped
10 leaves fresh basil, finely
   chopped
18 large scallops, rinsed, dried
   and halved

Separate the endive leaves and cut them lengthwise into thin strips. Cook them in a skillet in half the butter and a little salt and pepper until quite tender.

Melt the remaining butter in a clean skillet. Add the garlic and basil, and cook for a few minutes. Increase the heat to high, and sauté the scallops for 1-2 minutes in the mixture, first on one side and then on the other; taking care not to overcook them. Add a little salt and pepper. Serve the scallops in their sauce on a bed of warm endive.

STUFFED SQUID

I have a passion for squid, and enjoy cooking it in many different ways. Stuffing squid is not as complicated as it sounds – place the whiting mixture in a piping bag fitted with a large plain tip, and squeeze into the squid!

Serves 2 as a light lunch or 4 as an appetizer

INGREDIENTS
12 ounces whiting fillets, skinned
Scant 1 cup light cream
1 egg, beaten
Salt and freshly ground black
  pepper
½ carrot, diced
½ zucchini, peeled and diced
Scant 1 cup heavy cream
4 medium squid, well rinsed and
  dried inside and out, tentacles
  cut off
2½ cups fish stock
2 pinches saffron

To make the stuffing, purée the whiting fillets with 1 tablespoon light cream and the beaten egg in a blender or food processor. Add salt and pepper. Blanch the carrot and zucchini dice in boiling water for 2 minutes, and add to the whiting. Stir well to mix evenly. Whip the heavy cream, and fold it into the fish stuffing.

Stuff the squid with the whiting mixture, forcing it well down the tubes. Sew the ends up with fine kitchen thread or string to enclose the stuffing. Steam the squid for 15-20 minutes. Heat the stock in a saucepan, letting it reduce by three-quarters. Stir in the remaining light cream and the saffron. Let the sauce heat through, and then purée in a blender or food processor.

Remove the string from the squid, and serve with the sauce poured over.

MOULES MARINIÈRE

Moules Marinière, cooked in the style of the fisherman's wife, is one of the best-known of classic French dishes. It is simple to prepare, but care must be taken not to overcook the mussels. Shake the pan frequently – this mixes them up, and helps to prevent them from sticking.

Serves 4

INGREDIENTS
3½ quarts mussels, presoaked for
  1 hour in salted water
¼ cup butter
1 large onion, thinly sliced
2 cloves garlic, chopped
2 sprigs parsley
Salt and freshly ground black
  pepper
2½ pints dry white wine

To Serve
3 tablespoons freshly chopped
  parsley

Drain the mussels. Scrape off any persistent scales, and rinse the mussels thoroughly in cold running water. Remove any stringy beards. Melt half the butter in a large saucepan. Cook the onion, garlic, sprigs of parsley, salt and pepper for 4 minutes. Pour in the wine, and bring to a boil. Add the mussels. Cover the pan, and cook for about 8 minutes, or until all the shells have opened. Take the saucepan off the heat, and remove the mussels with a draining spoon. Discard any that have not opened. Keep the mussels warm.

Remove the sprig of parsley from the cooking liquor, and drain through a fine strainer. Return the liquor to the saucepan over a high heat, and bring it to a boil. Boil to reduce by at least one-third. Stir in the remaining butter and a little more salt and pepper to taste. Stir in the mussels, and serve hot, sprinkled with chopped parsley.

SCALLOPS AU GRATIN

Scallops require very gentle cooking – overcooking will toughen them, making them unpleasant to eat, when they should be a delectable treat. Do not use frozen scallops – they are seldom little more than mush once thawed.

Serves 4 as a fish appetizer or 2 as a light lunch

INGREDIENTS

4 large scallops
2 tablespoons olive oil
¼ cup butter
2 small shallots or 1 small onion, finely chopped
½ cup white wine
2 tablespoons heavy cream
2 egg yolks, lightly beaten
Salt and white pepper
⅓ cup grated Cheddar cheese
4 tablespoons fresh white bread crumbs

Allow one large scallop or two to three smaller scallops per person. Ask your fish supplier for four deep scallop shells in which to serve the appetizer.

Heat the oil and butter in a heavy skillet. Add the shallots, and cook slowly until soft. Slice the white of the scallops horizontally. Increase the heat. Add the white wine, then the sliced scallops, and cook briskly for 2-3 minutes. Slice the scallop corals, and add them to the pan, cooking for another minute. Remove the pan from the heat, and let cool slightly.

Add the cream to the scallops, then carefully stir in the lightly beaten egg yolks. Stir gently over a low heat until slightly thickened, then season lightly to taste. Divide the mixture between the scallop shells or four individual dishes, insuring that each has a fair share of coral.

Mix the cheese and bread crumbs together, and divide the mixture between the dishes. Place under a hot broiler until just beginning to brown. Serve the scallops immediately with brown bread and butter.

PROVENÇAL SQUID

*I love squid, but many people who try it fried are put off,
finding it chewy and tough. Slower cooking, such as in this
recipe, helps to tenderize the squid – this is the way I like to
cook it. I sometimes stew the squid for an hour or more –
they don't spoil; I think they get better!*

Serves 6

INGREDIENTS
Olive oil
5 pounds squid tubes, washed
   and cut into thin slices
1 teaspoon fennel seeds
   (optional)
5 onions, chopped
5 cloves garlic, chopped
1 teaspoon cayenne pepper
Bouquet garni
5 tomatoes, chopped
1¼ cups fish stock
1¼ cups dry white wine
Pinch of saffron
1 tablespoon heavy cream
Salt and freshly ground black
   pepper

Warm the oil in a skillet, and
cook the squid and fennel seeds
until all the juices evaporate.
Remove the squid with a
draining spoon, and add the
onion, garlic, cayenne pepper,
bouquet garni and tomatoes to
the pan. Stir well, and cook for a
few minutes. Add the stock and
the wine. Sprinkle in the saffron,
and stir well. Cook over a fairly
brisk heat until the sauce has
reduced by half. Return the squid
to the pan, and reduce the heat.
Cover the pan, and cook very
gently until the squid is tender –
about 20 minutes. Just before
serving, remove the bouquet
garni, and stir in the cream.
Check the seasoning and add a
little salt and pepper if necessary.

COQUILLES ST JACQUES

Scallops are a real treat. Frozen scallops look tempting until they defrost, at which stage they often turn into a soggy mush. Fresh scallops are vastly superior in both flavor and texture. Have the potato and scallop mixtures hot before broiling, so that the potato can brown quickly, and the scallops will not overcook.

Serves 4

INGREDIENTS
8 large scallops, cleaned
1¼ cups dry white wine
1 pound potatoes
1 egg yolk
⅓ cup butter
Salt and pepper - I use white
   pepper with scallops
½ onion, very finely chopped
1⅓ cups sliced mushrooms
⅓ cup all-purpose flour
⅔ cup heavy cream
Sprig of thyme
1 tablespoon freshly chopped
   parsley
½ cup shelled shrimp

4 scallop shells for serving

Remove and reserve the orange corals from the scallops. Slice the white parts into rounds, and poach them slowly in the dry white wine for 3-4 minutes (do not overcook the scallops, or they will become tough and rubbery). Strain the scallops, reserving the liquid. While the scallops are poaching, boil the potatoes in salted water until soft. Drain and mash the potatoes, adding the egg yolk, 2 tablespoons of the butter and seasoning. Set aside until required.

Melt the remaining butter in a small saucepan. Add the chopped onion, and cook for 2 minutes. Add the mushrooms, and cook for an additional 5 minutes or so. Sprinkle in the flour, and cook, stirring continuously, for 1 minute; then gradually add the scallop liquor, a little at a time. Mix to a smooth sauce, and cook for 2-3 minutes over a low heat before adding the cream and herbs. Season to taste, and add the shrimp and scallop corals. Heat slowly until almost boiling; then remove the thyme, and divide the mixture between the scallop shells.

Preheat the broiler. Pipe a little of the creamed potato around the edge of each scallop shell. Place the shells on the broiler rack and cook until the potato is lightly golden. Serve immediately.

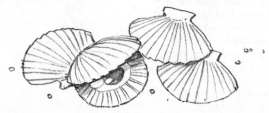

SOUFFLÉS ST JACQUES

These scallop soufflés combine two great traditions of French cuisine! Served with a tomato sauce, they both look and taste good!

Serves 4

INGREDIENTS

8 large or 16 small scallops, with roe attached
1¼ cups milk
3 tablespoons butter
⅓ cup all-purpose flour
Salt and white pepper
¼ teaspoon Dijon mustard
⅓ cup grated Cheddar cheese
4 eggs, separated

Tomato Sauce

14-ounce can of tomatoes
1 small onion, finely chopped
Bay leaf
Pinch of thyme
Sugar to taste
½ clove of garlic, crushed
1 tablespoon Worcestershire sauce
Salt and white pepper

Prepare the tomato sauce. Put all the ingredients into a small, heavy-bottomed saucepan, and bring to a boil. Simmer, half covered, for 20 minutes; then push the sauce through a strainer and set it aside.

Preheat the oven to 450°F. Poach the scallops in the milk for 3-5 minutes, depending on size. Remove the scallops from the milk, and set aside. Melt the butter in a pan until foaming. Remove from the heat, and beat in the flour. Cook over a low heat for about 1 minute, but do not let the mixture brown. Gradually beat in the milk in which the scallops were poached. Bring the mixture slowly to a boil, stirring continuously, and cook until thickened. Add the salt and pepper, mustard and grated cheese, then let the mixture cool slightly, before beating in the egg yolks.

Butter 4 ramekins or shell dishes. Slice the scallops horizontally, reserving 4 whole roes for garnish, and place the scallops in the bottom of the dishes. Beat the egg whites until stiff but not dry, and fold them into the cheese mixture. Spoon the soufflé into the prepared dishes, and place them on a baking sheet. Bake for about 10 minutes, or until well risen and set.

Reheat the tomato sauce while the soufflés are baking, and serve a little spooned over each soufflé, garnished with the reserved roes. Serve any remaining tomato sauce with the soufflés.

LOBSTER À LA CRÈME

This is a good way of making one lobster go a long way! A very rich and luxurious dish. Try using Calvados in place of the sherry.

Serves 2

INGREDIENTS

1 cold, boiled lobster
⅓ cup butter
Salt and freshly ground black
　pepper
Squeeze of lemon juice
Freshly grated nutmeg
1 small bunch tarragon, chopped
5 tablespoons dry sherry or
　Madeira
1¼ cups heavy cream
3 tablespoons dry white bread
　crumbs

Use a sharp knife to cut the lobster in half lengthwise. Remove all the meat from the tail. Crack the claws, and remove the meat from them; then extract as much as possible from the legs. Chop all the meat roughly.

Melt ¼ cup of the butter in a pan and sauté the lobster with the seasoning, lemon juice, nutmeg and tarragon. Add the sherry or Madeira to the pan. Heat and flame, shaking the pan until the flames die out.

Add the cream to the pan, and bring it to a boil; then boil for 5 minutes, or until the cream begins to thicken. Spoon the lobster cream into 2 individual dishes, and keep warm.

Melt the remaining butter in a small pan. Add the bread crumbs, and fry until browned. Scatter the bread crumbs over the lobster creams, and serve.

HARLEQUIN SCALLOPS

This particularly attractive dish is perfect for the special occasion. Take care when preparing the vegetables; they should be cut into very small cubes (brunoise). This way they remain quite crisp during cooking. The vegetables and scallops should be cooked over a very low heat. Queen scallops are very small, about 3 inches in diameter. Use if available, and serve in regular-size scallop shells for an attractive finish.

Serves 6

INGREDIENTS

54 fresh Queen scallops (or 24 regular-size scallops), on the half-shell
2 tablespoons olive oil
1 clove garlic, finely chopped
1 red bell pepper, seeded and cut into small dice
1 green bell pepper, seeded and cut into small dice
1 stalk celery, cut into small cubes
2 carrots, peeled and cut into small cubes
Salt and freshly ground black pepper
Pinch of thyme

Preheat the oven to 400°F. Slide all the scallops onto a plate. Keep cool.

Warm the oil in a large skillet, with the garlic, and add all the vegetables and the scallops. Cook in batches if necessary. Add a little salt and pepper and the thyme. Cook very slowly for a few minutes, stirring frequently, until the scallops are just done (opaque but slightly transparent in the center). The exact cooking time will depend on quantity and size. After cooking, the vegetables should still be quite crisp. Fill 36 regular-size (or 24 large) scallop shells with a little of the mixture, and then put them into the oven for about 5 minutes, to finish cooking. Serve piping hot.

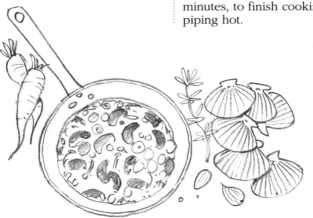

CRAB SALAD WITH RUM

A light salad with the Spanish influence of rum. This is best made with fresh crabmeat; canned crab is suitable for use when fresh crabs are out of season.

Serves 6

INGREDIENTS
2 avocados
Juice of 2 lemons
4 artichoke hearts
1 head lettuce, washed, dried and shredded
3 stalks celery, wiped, strings removed and sliced
12 ounces fresh crabmeat

Sauce
1 egg yolk
2 teaspoons Dijon mustard
⅔ cup oil
4 tablespoons light cream
3 tablespoons rum
1 tablespoon freshly chopped parsley
Salt and freshly ground black pepper

Peel the avocados, and, with a melon baller, scoop out the flesh. Dip the balls immediately into the lemon juice, and put them in a bowl in the refrigerator. Dice the artichoke hearts, and dip them into the lemon juice; then put them in the refrigerator with the avocado balls.

Make the sauce by beating the egg yolk with the mustard. Beat in the oil, drop by drop, then beat in the cream, rum, parsley, salt and pepper.

Place a small bed of lettuce on 6 individual plates, and top with the avocado, artichoke and the celery. Break up the crabmeat, and scatter it over the salad. Serve with the rum sauce spooned over.

SALADE AUX FRUITS DE MER

This is a celebration of seafood! It can be made with any combination of fish, but use a mixture of shellfish and white fish. Cook and eat the salad on the same day.

Serves 4

INGREDIENTS

Salad
8 scallops with roe attached
6 ounces monkfish
Lemon juice
Mussels
Cooked scampi
Cooked, shelled shrimps
1 head lettuce
1 head endive

Dressing
½ cup soft cheese
⅔ cup yogurt
Juice of 1 lemon
3 tablespoons milk
1 tablespoon Dijon mustard
1 tablespoon freshly chopped tarragon
1 tablespoon freshly chopped chives
1 tablespoon freshly chopped parsley
Salt and freshly ground black pepper

Poach the scallops and monkfish in a large pan in a little lemon juice with enough water to cover the fish. Cook for 5 minutes, then add the mussels. Cover the pan, and cook for an additional 3-4 minutes, until the mussels have opened. Remove all the fish from the pan, and let it cool completely. Add the scampi and shrimp, and chill.

Prepare the dressing by whisking all the ingredients together. Arrange the lettuce and endive on a large platter, and top with the chilled mixed fish. Spoon the dressing over, and serve immediately.

POULTRY & GAME

I actually find that I cannot go along with the traditional French country attitude toward poultry and game; well, that is until it reaches the kitchen table! Although I love the markets in towns and villages for fresh fruits and vegetables, I find the poultry stalls just a little too fresh – the birds are usually still alive! The stall holder might wring the bird's neck, but you will usually have to do the rest of the work yourself. I am afraid that, although I love food and thoroughly enjoy cooking, this is really too much for me, and I would rather pay the premium for a corn-fed, oven-ready chicken than pluck and draw a bird myself.

Fresh is Best

Of course, buying in the French way does insure that poultry is as fresh as possible, which is very important and a matter of great pride to the housewife and cook. The age of a bird in feather can easily be determined by feeling the beak – in a young bird it will be flexible, a good indication that the bird will be tender. Game birds, such as partridge and pheasants, need to be hung to develop their flavor.

An Empty Canvas

The marvellous thing about poultry, and especially chicken, is that it so readily accepts the flavors of other ingredients that are cooked with it. The great French gastronome Brillat-Savarin wrote that, "Poultry is for the cook what canvas is to the painter," and so it is, the starting-off point, the main ingredient of so many great and classic dishes. Some even relate to events in French history; Chicken Marengo was – so popular legend has it – created by Napoleon's chef to celebrate his victory against the Austrians at the Battle of Marengo. The battle was actually fought in Italy, just north of Genoa, so this classic French dish was first created from ingredients that were readily available in the Italian countryside: chicken, tomatoes, sherry or marsala, mushrooms, and eggs.

From the New World to the Old

Although I know that the French for turkey is *dindon*, I can actually think of very few classic French recipes that feature this bird. However, it must be popular in France as Brillat-Savarin described the turkey as "one of the finest gifts given to the Old World by the New." Escoffier described a meal of cream of pumpkin soup, followed by young spit-roasted turkey served with a large country sausage, enjoyed after a day's hunting. Perhaps this in itself epitomizes the French attitude to fine food, that the best and freshest ingredients need little embellishment and only simple dressing to make a truly memorable meal.

Duck or Duckling?

As duck can be somewhat fatty, it is often cooked with fruit to lighten the richness of the meat – duck with orange, duck with tart black cherries, duck with apples and Calvados. These dishes all stem from different regions of France; the southwest is home to the cherries, Normandy to apples, and this local association of ingredients can be seen in all the cookery of France. And when is a duck not a duck? When it's a duckling, and that is only for the first two months of its life. Duckling does not have the same gamy flavor as duck, and is best simply roasted.

Goose – the Gourmet's Delight

"Hissing and honking" is a colorful description of geese in a farmyard, and really very accurate! The ideal holiday image of a rural scene in southwest France, a major goose and *foie gras* area, is bound to feature geese in abundance. The meat itself is enjoyed casseroled or slowly roasted, but it is the liver, the *foie gras*, which is the delicacy of France.

Pheasant and Partridge – Real Country Cooking

The French country people eat a lot of game birds – pheasant, partridge, pigeon and woodcock. In the fall the men disappear for *La Palombière*, a weekend or longer of elaborate pigeon shooting involving decoys and many bottles of wine!

It is the wine produced in France that gives so much regional flavor to the country dishes based on game. "When in France, do as the French" – use the local wine to marinate the game birds, as all will be redolent of the area, blending the local produce together, however simply cooked, in the most spectacular way.

SLICED CHICKEN WITH FIGS

A new recipe that presents chicken in a new light – this recipe will delight all who taste it. Serve with Rice Pilaf.

Serves 6

INGREDIENTS
¼ cup butter
1 large chicken, boneless and cut into slices
1 small cinnamon stick
1¼ cups white wine
1¼ cups chicken stock
Pinch of saffron
15 coriander seeds
6 dried figs, each cut into 3
2 teaspoons honey
Salt and freshly ground black pepper

In a heavy skillet, heat the butter and the oil, and fry the chicken slices. Let brown slightly, then take the pan off the heat. Remove the chicken from the skillet, and keep it warm. Put the skillet back on the heat and add the cinnamon, wine, stock, saffron, coriander, figs, honey, salt and pepper. Stir well, and cook for 4 minutes. Return the chicken to the skillet. Cover the pan, and continue cooking for 20 minutes over a very low heat. Remove the chicken and the figs, and keep them warm. Remove and discard the cinnamon. Let the sauce boil until quite syrupy. Return the chicken and the figs to the skillet to heat, and serve.

BROILED CHICKEN WITH LIME

A perfect summer dish combining the refreshing tang of limes with the lightness of chicken. This recipe gives instructions for broiling the chicken and finishing it in the oven, but it could easily be barbecued if preferred.

Serves 4

INGREDIENTS
2 × 2 pound chickens
Salt and freshly ground black
  pepper
1 tablespoon freshly chopped
  basil
⅓ cup olive oil
4 limes
Sugar to taste

Remove the leg and wing tips from the chickens, and discard them. Split the chicken in half, cutting away the backbone completely and discarding it. Bend the chicken legs back to loosen the ball and socket joints, and flatten each half of the chickens by hitting it with the flat side of a cleaver or a rolling pin. Season the chicken on both sides with salt and pepper, and sprinkle with the basil. Place the chicken halves in a shallow dish, and pour over 2 tablespoons of olive oil. Squeeze the juice from 2 of the limes over the chicken. Cover the dish, and let the chicken marinate in the refrigerator for 4 hours.

Heat the broiler to its highest setting, and preheat the oven to 375°F. Remove the chicken from the marinade, and place it in the broiler pan. Cook one side until golden-brown, then turn the pieces over. Drizzle with 1 tablespoon of olive oil and brown the other side.

Place the chicken in a roasting pan. Drizzle with the remaining oil, and roast in the oven for about 25 minutes. Peel the remaining limes, and slice them thinly. When the chicken is cooked, place the lime slices on top of the chicken, and sprinkle with a little sugar. Place under a hot broiler for a few minutes to caramelize the sugar and cook the limes. Transfer to a warmed serving dish. Heat any remaining marinade and the cooking juices together briefly; then spoon over the chicken, and serve immediately.

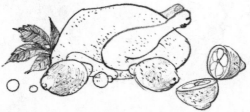

PROVENÇAL CHICKEN

A classic dish from Provence in the south of France. The chicken is cooked with herbs, tomatoes, garlic, olives and anchovies for the authentic flavor of the Mediterranean.

Serves 4

INGREDIENTS

1 teaspoon salt
1 teaspoon black pepper
1 clove garlic, crushed
3 tablespoons olive oil
4-pound chicken, cut into 8 pieces
1 medium onion, finely chopped
8 ounces cup mushrooms
¼ cup all-purpose flour
¾ cup white wine
½ cup chicken stock
3 tomatoes, skinned, seeded and roughly chopped
1 tablespoon fresh basil leaves, torn
6 black olives, halved and pitted
2-ounce can anchovy fillets

Preheat the oven to 325°F. Rub the salt, pepper and crushed garlic over the chicken pieces, and set them aside. Heat the oil in a large flame-proof casserole. When hot, sauté the chicken pieces, turning them frequently, until they are evenly browned. Reduce the heat, and add the chopped onion. Cover the casserole, and cook for about 20-25 minutes, until the chicken is tender. Transfer the chicken to an ovenproof casserole, and keep it warm in the oven while making the sauce.

Halve the mushrooms, and add them to the flameproof casserole. Sauté for 2-3 minutes. Stir in the flour, and cook for 30 seconds before gradually pouring in the wine and stock. Bring the sauce to a boil, stirring constantly. Add the tomatoes, basil and olives. Chop half the anchovies, and add them to the casserole. Return the mixture to a boil; then reduce the heat and simmer for 10 minutes. Remove the chicken from the oven, and coat it with the sauce; then garnish with the remaining anchovies. Serve immediately.

NORMANDY-STYLE CHICKEN POULET SAUTÉ VALLÉE D'AUGE

This is a classic dish of Normandy – chicken in a rich creamy sauce flavored with apples and Calvados, the famed apple brandy of the region. The chicken is garnished in a traditional way, with caramelized apple slices.

Serves 4

INGREDIENTS

¼ cup butter
2 tablespoons oil
3-pound chicken, jointed into
  eight pieces
4 tablespoons Calvados
6 tablespoons chicken stock
2 apples, peeled, cored and
  roughly chopped
1 shallot, finely chopped
2 stalks celery, finely chopped
1 teaspoon freshly chopped
  thyme

2 egg yolks, lightly beaten
⅓ cup heavy cream
Salt and white pepper

Garnish
2 tablespoons butter
2 apples, quartered, cored and
  diced
Sugar
1 bunch watercress or small
  parsley sprigs

Heat half the butter and all of the oil in a large sauté pan over a medium heat. When the foam begins to subside, add the chicken, a few pieces at a time, and brown on all sides – place the chicken skin-side down first. When all the chicken is browned, remove it from the pan, and drain off most of the fat; then return the chicken to the pan.

Pour the Calvados into a small saucepan, and warm it slowly over a low heat. Ignite it with a match, and pour it, while still flaming, over the chicken. Shake the pan gently until the flames subside. If the Calvados should flare up, cover the pan immediately with a lid. Pour in the stock, and scrape any browned chicken juices up from the bottom of the pan. Set the chicken aside.

Melt the remaining butter in a small saucepan or skillet. Cook the chopped apples, shallot, celery and thyme for about 10 minutes, or until soft but not browned. Spoon the mixture over the chicken and return the pan to a high heat. Bring to a boil, then reduce the heat. Cover the pan and simmer for 50 minutes.

Beat the egg yolks and cream together, and, with a whisk, gradually beat in some of the hot sauce from the chicken. Pour the mixture back into a saucepan, and cook over a low heat for 2-3 minutes, stirring constantly, until the sauce thickens and coats the back of a spoon. Season the sauce with salt and white pepper, and set aside while preparing the garnish.

Put the butter for the garnish in a small skillet, and, when foaming, add the diced apples. Toss over a high heat until the apples are beginning to soften. Add a little sugar, and cook until the sugar begins to caramelize.

To serve, coat the chicken with the sauce, and garnish with watercress or parsley. Spoon the caramelized apples over the chicken.

CHICKEN WITH RICE
POULET AU RIZ

This is a classic dish from the Alsace area of France. The chicken is flavored with a variety of vegetables, and then cream is added for a rich, smooth sauce. Cook the rice in your favorite way, but it is usually served boiled.

Serves 6

INGREDIENTS

1 large boiling chicken, cleaned
　and dried
Juice of 1 lemon
1 onion, chopped
1 carrot, chopped
1 leek, chopped
1 stalk celery, finely chopped
Bouquet garni
¼ cup butter
½ cup flour
1¼ cups heavy cream
Salt and freshly ground black
　pepper
Cooked long-grain rice for
　serving

Put the chicken in a large saucepan, and cover it with cold water. Bring to a boil; as soon as the water is boiling well, remove the chicken, and drain well. Cut up the chicken, separating the wings, thighs and the breasts. Sprinkle the lemon juice over the meat. Break up the carcass.

Put the carcass bones back into the saucepan, and cover with fresh water. Add all the vegetables, the bouquet garni and chicken pieces. Bring to a boil; then cover the pan, and reduce the heat. Simmer until the meat is tender. Remove the pieces of chicken, and keep them warm. Boil what remains in the saucepan and let it reduce, skimming off any fat that rises to the top. Drain the sauce through a fine strainer and discard everything but the strained liquor.

Melt the butter in another saucepan, and stir in the flour. Stir in the juices, and continue stirring until the sauce boils and thickens. Cook for a few minutes more, and then stir in the cream. Add salt and pepper. Serve the pieces of chicken on a bed of boiled rice with the sauce poured over.

CHICKEN MARENGO

This was one of the first classic French dishes that I learned when I was studying food at college! Created to celebrate Napoleon's victory at the Battle of Marengo, it reflects the ingredients that were available around the battle site, which was actually in Italy!

Serves 4

INGREDIENTS
¼ cup butter
5 tablespoons olive oil
3-pound chicken, cut into 8
  pieces
2 onions, finely sliced
1-2 plump cloves garlic, crushed
1 tablespoon all-purpose flour
14-ounce can chopped tomatoes
2 cups dark chicken stock
Salt and freshly ground black
  pepper
4 ounces button mushrooms
1 truffle, sliced (optional)
Oil
4 small slices bread, crusts
  removed
4 eggs
Freshly chopped parsley to
  garnish

Heat the butter with 2 tablespoons of the olive oil in a large skillet or sauté pan. Add the chicken pieces, a few at a time, and brown on all sides. Remove the chicken with a draining spoon and set aside.

Add the onions and garlic to the pan, and cook slowly until softened. Increase the heat, and brown the onions; then add the flour, and cook for about 1 minute, until browned. Add the tomatoes and stock – ⅔ cup of the stock may be replaced with sherry if preferred. Bring the sauce to a boil, stirring continuously, then season to taste with salt and pepper.

Return the chicken to the pan, and add the mushrooms and truffle, if using. Cover the pan, and simmer slowly for 1 hour, or until the chicken is tender.

Heat a little oil in a skillet. Cut the bread into triangles, and fry lightly until golden-brown. Fry the eggs separately. Season the chicken, if necessary. Transfer the chicken pieces to a serving dish, and garnish with the fried bread and eggs. Sprinkle with chopped parsley, and serve.

CHICKEN WITH TARRAGON SAUCE

Muscat de Beaumes de Venise gives a sweet richness of flavor to the popular marriage of poultry and tarragon. Insure that the tarragon is French and not Russian – the former has a much finer flavor.

Serves 6

INGREDIENTS

3 tablespoons oil
½ cup butter
2 chickens, jointed
6 shallots, chopped
1 carrot, chopped
3 sprigs fresh tarragon
⅓ cup Muscat de Beaumes de Venise
⅔ cup white wine
1¼ cups chicken stock
Salt and freshly ground black pepper
1 tablespoon cornstarch mixed with 1 tablespoon water (optional)
2 tablespoons freshly chopped tarragon

Heat the oil and half the butter in a large flameproof casserole. Add the chicken pieces, and brown on all sides. Transfer the chicken to a plate. Add the remaining butter to the casserole, and cook the shallots, carrot and sprigs of tarragon for 5 minutes. Slide the chicken pieces back into the casserole, and stir well; then stir in the Muscat. Add the wine and chicken stock, salt and pepper, and stir well. Bring to a boil. Cover the casserole, then reduce the heat, and simmer for 30 minutes. Add a little water if necessary during cooking.

When the chicken pieces are cooked, remove them and place in a warmed serving dish. Bring the sauce to a boil, and let it reduce and thicken. If necessary, stir in the cornstarch and water mixture, stirring continuously until the sauce has boiled and thickened. Season the sauce, and serve it poured over the chicken. Sprinkle with the chopped tarragon.

CHICKEN ALSACE

*This is a very rich recipe from Alsace. Use fine kitchen string
to tie up the packages of chicken if a caulfat is not available.
Thicken the sauce if necessary with cornstarch – I prefer not
to if at all possible.*

Serves 6

INGREDIENTS
1 large chicken, boneless and
 cleaned (reserve the carcass,
 and liver)
1 egg, beaten
Scant 1 cup heavy cream,
 whipped
Salt and freshly ground black
 pepper
2 tablespoons Cognac
2 tablespoons heavy cream
1 sheet of caulfat
¼ cup plus 1 tablespoon butter
1 carrot, shredded
1 leek (white part only), grated
1 onion, grated
⅔ cup white wine
2 tablespoons light cream
3 tablespoons oil
2 ounces raw foie gras (duck or
 goose liver)

Preheat the oven to 400°F.
Remove one of the chicken
breasts, and, in a blender or food
processor, combine it with the
chicken liver, egg, whipped
cream, salt and pepper. Press this
mixture through a fine strainer
and add half the Cognac and the
2 tablespoons of heavy cream to
form a stiff paste. Spread this

paste over the chicken meat, and
then roll up neatly. Cut the
chicken into 6 pieces, and cut
the caulfat to fit around each
piece. If necessary, the ends can
be secured by tying them up
with fine kitchen string. Keep the
chicken in a cool place.

Melt the ¼ cup of butter in a
heavy skillet and cook the carrot,
leek, onion and broken up
carcass for 5 minutes. Add the
white wine, and cover the bones
with water. Bring to a boil, and
let cook until the sauce reduces a
little and thickens slightly. Press
through a fine strainer, then put
the sauce back in a saucepan
over quite a high heat. Stir in the
light cream and the remaining
Cognac, and let reduce until
quite thick.

Heat the 1 tablespoon of butter
with the oil in a heavy skillet,
and brown the pieces of meat on
all sides. Roast in the oven for
about 30 minutes. Just before
serving, whisk the foie gras into
the sauce, blending it with a
hand mixer. Cut the meat into
neat slices, discarding any string,
and pour the sauce over.

CHICKEN IN RED WINE
COQ AU VIN

This dish, under its French name of Coq au Vin, is one of the most famous chicken recipes in the world. It is hearty, rich and warming – a perfect cold weather classic and definitely not a dish for the summer!

Serves 4

INGREDIENTS

16 thick-cut bacon slices
2 cups water
12-16 button onions or shallots, quartered if large
2 tablespoons butter
8 ounces button mushrooms
3-pound chicken, cut into eight pieces
2 cups dry red wine

3 tablespoons brandy
Bouquet garni
1 clove garlic, crushed
3 tablespoons all-purpose flour
2 cups chicken stock
Salt and freshly ground black pepper
4 slices of bread, crusts removed
Oil for frying
2 tablespoons freshly chopped parsley

Preheat the oven to 350°F. Cut the bacon into strips about ¼ inch thick. Bring a pan of water to a boil, and blanch the bacon by simmering it for 5 minutes in the water. Remove the bacon with a draining spoon, and dry it on paper towels. Bring the water to a boil again, and drop in the onions. Let them boil rapidly for 2-3 minutes; then plunge them into cold water, and peel them. Set the onions aside with the bacon.

Melt half the butter in a large skillet over a moderate heat, and add the bacon and onions. Fry over a high heat, stirring frequently and shaking the pan, until the bacon and onions are golden-brown. Remove them with a draining spoon, and drain on paper towels. Add the remaining butter to the saucepan, and cook the mushrooms for 1-2 minutes. Remove them, and set them aside with the onions and bacon.

Reheat the skillet, and brown the chicken, a few pieces at a time. When all the pieces are browned, transfer the chicken to a large ovenproof casserole. Pour the wine into a small saucepan, and boil it until reduced to about 1¼ cups. Pour the brandy into a small saucepan, and warm it over a low heat. Ignite with a match, and pour the brandy (while still flaming) over the chicken. Shake the casserole carefully until the flames die down. If the brandy should flare up, cover the casserole quickly with the lid. Add the bouquet garni and garlic to the casserole.

Pour off all but 1 tablespoon of fat from the skillet in which the vegetables were cooked, and stir in the flour. Cook over a low heat, scraping any of the browned chicken juices from the bottom of the pan. Pour in the reduced wine, and add the stock. Bring the sauce to a boil over a high heat, stirring constantly until thickened. Strain over the chicken in the casserole, and cover the dish tightly.

Place in the oven, and cook for 20 minutes. Add the bacon, onions and mushrooms, and continue cooking for an additional 15-20 minutes, or until the chicken is tender. Remove the bouquet garni, and season with salt and pepper.

Cut each slice of bread into 4 triangles. Heat enough oil in a large skillet to cover the bread. When the oil is very hot, add the bread triangles, two at a time, and fry until golden-brown and crisp. Drain on paper towels.

To serve, arrange the chicken in a deep dish, and coat with the sauce. Top with the vegetables, then arrange the fried bread around the outside of the dish. Sprinkle with freshly chopped parsley.

CHICKEN FRICASSÉE

This is a rich, creamy, classic white stew. It is thickened with a mixture of egg yolks and cream, a mixture which is called a liaison. Chicken fricassée is usually served with boiled rice, and I would serve a tossed green salad after the chicken.

INGREDIENTS
¼ cup butter
3-pound chicken, quartered and skinned
¼ cup all-purpose flour
2½ cups chicken stock
Juice and grated rind of ½ a lemon
Bouquet garni
12-16 small onions, peeled
12 ounces small button mushrooms
2 egg yolks
⅓ cup heavy cream
3 tablespoons milk (optional)
Salt and white pepper
2 tablespoons freshly chopped parsley and thyme, mixed
Lemon slices to garnish

Melt 3 tablespoons of the butter in a large sauté pan or skillet. Add the chicken in one layer, and cook over a low heat for about 5 minutes, or until the chicken is no longer pink. Do not let the chicken brown. Cook the chicken in two batches if necessary. When the chicken has lost its pinkness, remove it from the pan, and set it aside. Stir the flour into the butter remaining in the pan, and cook over a very low heat, stirring continuously, for about 1 minute, or until a pale straw color.

Remove the pan from the heat, and gradually beat in the chicken stock. When blended smoothly, add the lemon juice and peel. Return the pan to the heat, and bring the sauce to a boil, whisking continuously. Reduce the heat and let the sauce simmer for 1 minute.

Return the chicken to the pan with any juices that have accumulated, and add the bouquet garni. The sauce should almost cover the chicken. If it does not, add more stock or water. Bring to a boil; cover the pan, and reduce the heat. Let the chicken simmer gently for 30 minutes.

Meanwhile, melt the remaining butter in a small skillet. Add the onions; cover the pan, and cook very slowly for 10 minutes. Do not let the onions brown. Remove the onions from the pan with a draining spoon, and add them to the chicken. Cook the mushrooms in the skillet in the remaining butter for 2 minutes; then set them aside, and add them to the chicken 10 minutes before the end of cooking.

Test the chicken by piercing a thigh portion with a sharp knife. If the juices run clear, the chicken is cooked. Transfer the chicken and vegetables to a serving dish, and discard the bouquet garni. Skim the sauce of any fat, and boil it rapidly to reduce by almost half.

Blend the egg yolks and cream together, and whisk in several spoonfuls of the hot sauce. Return the egg yolk and cream mixture to the remaining sauce, and cook slowly for 2-3 minutes. Stir the sauce continuously and do not let it boil – you will get separated scrambled eggs! If it is very thick, add a little milk. Adjust the seasoning, and stir in the parsley and thyme. Spoon the sauce over the chicken in the serving dish. Garnish with lemon slices before serving.

111

TURKEY WITH FRESH TARRAGON

Turkey and tarragon go together very well – I often serve cold turkey in a tarragon mayonnaise. I would serve this creamy turkey dish with boiled rice.

Serves 6

INGREDIENTS

3 large turkey breasts, about 2-2¼ pounds in total
Salt and freshly ground black pepper
2 tablespoons oil
1 knob of butter
2 tablespoons freshly chopped tarragon
2 tablespoons port
1¼ cups chicken stock
1 tablespoon cornstarch, dissolved in 1 tablespoon water
6 tablespoons heavy cream

Preheat the oven to 375°F. Sprinkle the turkey breasts with salt and pepper, and then cook them in a flameproof casserole dish in the oil and butter until lightly browned. Pour off any excess fat. Add the tarragon, port and stock, and stir well. Bring to a boil; then reduce the heat very slightly, and let cook until the juices in the casserole have reduced by about a third. Cover the casserole, and place in the oven to finish cooking the turkey – this will take about 20 minutes. When the turkey is cooked through and ready to serve, remove the breasts, and set aside. Stir the dissolved cornstarch into the juices, stirring continuously, and heat on the stove top until the sauce thickens. Stir in the cream. Cut the breasts into thin slices and serve with the sauce poured over.

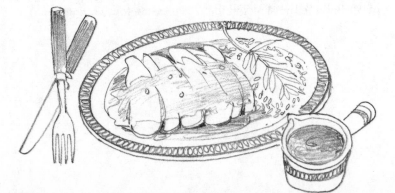

RABBIT IN MUSTARD SAUCE

Rabbit is popular in France, especially in traditional country dishes. It is light, lacking much of the heaviness of other dishes which are often flavored and enriched with cream. Rabbit is often dressed with mustard – Dijon is still the home of the French mustard trade, producing around 50 percent of the world's mustard.

Serves 4

INGREDIENTS

4 pounds rabbit, cleaned and cut into pieces
4 tablespoons Dijon mustard
2 tablespoons butter
1 tablespoon oil
1 medium onion, finely chopped
¼ cup all-purpose flour
1 tablespoon freshly chopped thyme
1 teaspoon fresh rosemary
2 cups dry cider
Salt and freshly ground black pepper

Smear the rabbit pieces with the mustard, and set aside for 2-3 hours to absorb the flavor. Heat the butter and oil together in a large skillet. When the foam subsides, fry the rabbit pieces, a few at a time, until golden-brown, then transfer them to a flameproof casserole dish. Add the chopped onion to the skillet, adding a little more oil if necessary. Fry the onion until soft, and then add the flour and herbs, stirring continuously. Cook for 1-2 minutes over a low heat, then add the cider. Stir the sauce well, and bring it to a boil. Season to taste, then pour the thickened sauce over the rabbit pieces. Cover the casserole, and simmer gently for 45-60 minutes, until tender.

This dish is delicious served with buttered noodles, and followed by a green salad. French bread could be served in place of the pasta, to mop up all the delicious juices.

HUNTER'S RABBIT
LAPIN CHASSEUR

Rabbit is an excellent country food to cook "chasseur" – in the style of the hunter. Such dishes always include mushrooms, and sometimes bacon or tomatoes.

Serves 6

INGREDIENTS
1 rabbit, cleaned
½ cup diced smoked bacon
1 onion, chopped
1¼ cups white wine
Bouquet garni
Pinch of nutmeg
Salt and freshly ground black
  pepper
3 cups sliced mushrooms
1 tablespoon butter
1 tablespoon flour
1 tablespoon freshly chopped
  parsley

Bone the rabbit, and cut the meat into small pieces. Cook the bacon in a flameproof casserole on the stove top, without adding any extra fat, until the fat from the bacon is running. Stir in the rabbit pieces, and add the onion; continue cooking until the onion is soft. Pour in the wine and 1¼ cups water. Add the bouquet garni, nutmeg, salt and pepper, and bring to a boil. Cover the pan, and reduce the heat. Simmer for 30 minutes. Add the mushrooms, and then simmer slowly for an additional 15 minutes.

Just before serving, beat together the butter and the flour. Gradually whisk this into the sauce, boiling the sauce between each addition, until the sauce thickens to the required consistency. Serve the rabbit with the parsley sprinkled over.

DUCK BREAST WITH GREEN PEPPERCORN SAUCE

Green peppercorns are often served with beef steaks either in a sauce or crushed over the meat. They make an unusual and delicious sauce for duck – spicy and rich.

Serves 6

INGREDIENTS

2¼ pounds duck or poultry
  bones and trimmings
1 tablespoon oil
1 onion, finely chopped
1 carrot, finely chopped
1 leek, finely chopped
1¼ cups white wine
Salt and freshly ground black
  pepper
1 teaspoon thyme
1 bay leaf
3 large duck breasts
1 tablespoon green peppercorns
1 tablespoon Cognac
Scant 1 cup heavy cream

Preheat the oven to 400°F. Break up the bones, and cook them in the oil in a heavy skillet with the trimmings, 2 tablespoons water, the onion, carrot and leek for 5 minutes. Add the white wine and enough water to cover. Add salt and pepper, the thyme and bay leaf, and bring to a boil. Let reduce by half. When the sauce has reduced, drain it through a fine strainer, then return it to the heat and reduce a little more.

Score the skin on the duck breasts. In a clean skillet, seal the breasts over a high heat, skin-side first. When sealed on all sides, continue cooking the duck in the oven until just a thin line of pink is visible in the center of the breasts – this takes about 10-15 minutes. Set the breasts aside, and keep them warm.

Sauté the peppercorns in the fat from the duck breasts for 1 minute. Add the Cognac, then stir in the reduced sauce. Let this reduce a little more, then stir in the cream. Season to taste. Cut the breasts into slices, and serve with the sauce poured over.

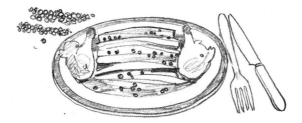

BRAISED DUCKLING WITH TURNIP SAUCE

This is a most unusual but delicious dish. Turnips are slightly peppery and complement the duckling well. I find that the best way to extract the juice from the turnips is to grate them, and then to squeeze the juice out in your clenched fist.

Serves 4-6

INGREDIENTS
1 large duckling
3 pounds turnips, peeled and
  sliced
3 onions, sliced
Juice of 3 large turnips
1 clove garlic
Bouquet garni
Salt and freshly ground black
  pepper

Cut the duckling into pieces, then brown them in a casserole without adding any more fat. Add the sliced turnips, and continue cooking. When the turnip has become slightly transparent, add 2 tablespoons water, the onions, turnip juice, garlic, bouquet garni, salt and pepper. Cook over a very low heat for 20-30 minutes. Remove the bouquet garni, the duckling pieces and the turnip.

Combine the juices in a blender or food processor until smooth. Add up to half of the cooked turnip, a little at a time, to thicken the sauce. Serve the duckling pieces interlaced with the remaining turnip slices, and pour the sauce around the edge of the dish.

DUCK IN ORANGE SAUCE
DUCK À L'ORANGE

Second only to Peking Duck, a classic Chinese dish, this must be one of the most famous recipes for duck in the world. I much prefer it to duck with black cherries – all too often jam is used in that sauce, making it far too sweet for my taste.

Serves 6

INGREDIENTS

8 oranges, washed and dried
Scant ⅓ cup butter
1 large duck, prepared and cut
 into pieces
1 onion, finely chopped
1 carrot, scraped and shredded
1 tablespoon vinegar
1 tablespoon cornstarch,
 dissolved in 1 tablespoon
 water
Salt and freshly ground black
 pepper

Thinly peel 2 of the oranges with a potato peeler, and cut the peel into fine strips. Blanch the strips in boiling water for a few minutes; drain well and set aside. Retain the oranges for their juice. Peel 4 more oranges, removing all the white pith and cut the flesh into thick slices.

Melt ¼ cup of the butter in a heavy casserole, and brown the duck pieces on all sides. Reduce the heat, and add the onion, carrot and 2 tablespoons of water. Cover the pan, and cook for about 30 minutes, turning the duck pieces occasionally. Add a little water if necessary during cooking. Remove the duck pieces from the casserole, and wrap them tightly in foil to keep warm. Drain the juices from the casserole through a fine strainer into a clean saucepan. Squeeze the juice of the peeled oranges and the 2 remaining oranges. Add this to the strained casserole juices, and stir well. Add the vinegar and the orange strips. Cook over a low heat for a few minutes. Add the dissolved cornstarch, stirring continuously, until the sauce boils and begins to thicken. Remove from the heat and season to taste. Cut the meat from the duck bones, and place it on a serving dish. Cook the orange slices in the remaining butter in a small pan until they have taken on a little color. Add them to the sauce, and stir. Serve the sauce poured over the duck.

QUAIL WITH GRAPES

Quail are becoming more popular, and some supermarkets now stock them "oven-ready." The grapes give a fragrance to the sauce, which should be served over or around the quail, sitting in splendor on freshly cooked croûtes or toasts.

Serves 6

INGREDIENTS

6 quail, cleaned and trussed
½ cup butter
2 tablespoons oil
⅔ cup Madeira
3 cups seedless green grapes
2½ cups rich chicken stock
Salt and freshly ground black
  pepper
6 slices of white bread

Preheat the oven to 400°F. Melt a knob of the butter with 1 tablespoon of the oil in a skillet, and slowly brown the birds all over. Remove from the pan, and finish cooking in a roasting pan the hot oven for about 15 minutes. Pour off any excess fat from the roasting pan and add the Madeira. Heat until almost evaporated, stirring up any meaty sediment from the bottom of the pan. Add the grapes, and then stir in the stock. Let reduce to a syrupy consistency.

Remove the grapes using a draining spoon. Stir in the remaining butter, reserving a knob for the toasts, and season the sauce with salt and pepper. Purée in a blender or food processor, then replace the grapes.

Fry the bread in the knob of butter with the remaining oil. Serve the quail on the toasts, with the sauce poured over.

PARTRIDGES WITH ARMAGNAC

This classic recipe combines many fine ingredients;
partridges, cream, a truffle and Armagnac. It is luxurious,
to be served on special occasions.

Serves 6

Ingredients

3 young partridges, cleaned
   (retain the gizzards and the
   livers)
¼ cup butter
1 tablespoon olive oil
4 tablespoons Armagnac
½ cup heavy cream
1 truffle, crumbled
Salt and freshly ground black
   pepper

Preheat the oven to 400°F. Truss the birds with kitchen string. Heat 1½ tablespoons of the butter with the oil in a heavy pan, and brown the birds on all sides. Remove them from the saucepan (retain the juices), and finish cooking in the oven for 20 minutes.

When the birds are cooked, cut off the wings, thighs and the breasts. Set them aside, and keep them warm.

Crush the carcasses, and put them back into the saucepan containing the juices. Add the gizzards and livers. Place over a high heat, and add the Armagnac and the cream. Stir well. Remove from the heat, and drain through a fine strainer. Add the crumbled truffle, and whisk in the remaining butter. Combine in a blender or food processor until smooth, then season to taste.

Cut the partridges into slices, and serve with the sauce poured over.

GUINEA FOWL CASSEROLE

Guinea fowl are very popular in the central regions of France.

Serves 6

INGREDIENTS
½ pound diced smoked bacon
1 onion, diced
3 carrots, diced
1 stalk celery, diced
2 turnips, diced
2 large, young guinea fowl, cleaned, dried and cut into 4
2 teaspoons all-purpose flour
⅔ cup red wine
2½ cups diced mushrooms
2 tablespoons heavy cream
Salt and freshly ground black pepper

Preheat the oven to 375°F. Cook the bacon slowly in a large flameproof casserole until the fat begins to run, then add the onion, carrots, celery and turnips. Cook until all the vegetables have turned slightly brown. Using a draining spoon, transfer all the above ingredients from the casserole to a plate. Add the guinea fowl pieces to the casserole. Increase the heat, and brown on all sides. Sprinkle with the flour, stir and cook for 1 minute. Add the wine, stirring continuously, then return all the ingredients from the plate. Stir in a scant cup of water, and add the mushrooms. Cover and cook in the oven until the fowl is cooked through, stirring from time to time – this will take about 30-40 minutes. Remove the guinea fowl, and the vegetables, then stir in the cream and drain the sauce through a fine strainer. Combine the sauce with a hand mixer or in a blender. Season with a little salt and pepper. Serve the fowl on top of the blended sauce, covered with the mushroom and vegetable mixture.

PHEASANT WITH APPLES

*This dish could hail from nowhere but Normandy – it
contains pheasant, apples, Calvados and cream. Don't be
tempted to overcook pheasant, which can easily become dry.*

Serves 6

INGREDIENTS

¼ cup butter
2 tablespoons oil
2 thick slices smoked bacon,
  diced
1 onion, finely chopped
1 large pheasant, wiped and cut
  into 6 pieces
5 cooking apples, peeled and
  sliced
3 tablespoons Calvados
Scant 1 cup heavy cream
Salt and freshly ground black
  pepper

Preheat the oven to 375°F. Heat
the butter with the oil in a large
skillet. Add the bacon and onion,
and cook until soft. Remove with
a draining spoon, and keep on a
plate. Brown the pheasant pieces
in the same skillet. Transfer to
the plate when they are well
colored and sealed. Add the
sliced apples to the same skillet,
and season with salt and pepper;
cook until browned. Add the
cooked apple to the plate, then
wipe the skillet with paper
towels.

Put all the cooked ingredients
back into the clean skillet. Add
the Calvados and ⅔ cup of water.
Cover the skillet, and cook over
a low heat for 10 minutes. Pour
all the contents of the skillet into
a flameproof casserole; cover and
finish cooking in the oven for 15
minutes. Stir in the cream
halfway through cooking. Take
the casserole out of the oven,
and remove the pheasant. Let the
sauce reduce slightly over a fairly
high heat, then purée in a
blender or food processor. Put
the sauce and pheasant pieces
back into the casserole. Taste
and adjust the seasoning if
necessary, and serve
immediately.

MEAT

The French really enjoy all their food, not least meat. They pride themselves on their beef, they eat a lot of lamb, they still enjoy veal despite it being less fashionable now in so many other countries, and they eat a great deal of offal.

Charcuterie – a Great French Tradition

The French not only enjoy their meat roasted, casseroled and braised, they are also a nation of sausage lovers, enjoying countless varieties of *saucisses sèches*, the French answer to the salami of Italy and the smoked sausages of Germany.

The charcuterie center of France is Lyons in Burgundy. The term charcuterie (from *chair cuite* or cold meat) actually covers two groups of foods: prepared foods such as salads, pies, and quiches, and any product of the pig. It is the latter group that is most commonly referred to as charcuterie. *Cervelas, Jésus salami, saucisson à l'ail* and the many hams cured in France are all rightfully placed among the best cold meat products in the world, and the marvelous pâtés produced throughout France are certainly internationally acclaimed. Fresh hams take much of their flavor from the local grazing of the pigs – those fed on acorns in oak woods under the ancient right of *pannage* have the most wonderful flavor while, of the air-dried hams, the *Jambon de Bayonne* is probably my favorite.

A trip to the local market will reveal the local sausage specialties, many of which do not have recognizable names. I just choose one which the locals are buying, after tasting the readily proffered sample. I love the French sausage stands which are little more than a broom handle with the sausage draped over – I had one when I owned a deli and it was a great selling feature; customers just decide how many inches of sausage they want, and it is cut for them.

Most of the charcuterie products that I have described here are eaten cold, the preserved sausages sliced thinly and served with a glass of wine before a meal, and many other products are simply served with toast or hot potatoes. Recipes for these foods don't exist – they are just to be enjoyed as they are. Why, then, have I written about them at such length in this introduction to French meat cookery? Well, charcuterie is so much a part of French life that it demands to be included in any description of meat in French cuisine.

Regional Pride
Although many dishes are regarded with fierce regional pride, careful examination will reveal that some of the dishes best known to those of us living outside France are simply regional variations on the same theme. For example, the local wine may change a beef stew from *Bourguignon* when cooked in Burgundy, to *Bordelais* when cooked in Bordeaux with the addition of marrow bone. I find the best wine for a *daube*, a beef stew from Provence, is a Cotês du Rhône, again the *vin du pays*.

Vive la Différence!
Casseroles and stews are prepared in pretty much the same way the world over – the best are always cooked slowly with

sympathetic seasoning to bring out the flavors in the meat. The French make time to cook their dishes slowly, showing real dedication and care in their preparation and cooking. You just cannot hurry something good!

The French are most particular that their meat should be well marbled with fat, but they trim most of the fat surrounding a piece of meat away. Lamb chops with the fat cut away from the bones right down to the eye of the meat are referred to as *"French trimmed"* or *"Frenched,"* and this method of preparation is also applied to roasts. The meat is also cooked very quickly at a very high temperature (usually 425°F, producing a well cooked outside and a very pink, rare center. This is exactly how the French like their meat, but it is not to everyone's taste – most medium to well-cooked meats need longer cooking at a more moderate temperature. This high temperature roasting produces a great deal of splatter in the oven, which is why more ovens with catalytic cleaning (a high temperature method of burning any spatter off the oven walls) are sold in France than in any other country in Europe!

PORK TENDERLOIN WITH PRUNES

An easy meal to prepare and cook, with a delicious, slightly sweet sauce.

Serves 6

INGREDIENTS
2¼ pounds pork tenderloin
20 slices smoked bacon
1 tablespoon olive oil
1 shallot, finely chopped
½ carrot, finely chopped
2 tablespoons port
1¼ cups chicken stock
8 ounces pitted prunes
Salt and freshly ground black
  pepper

Preheat the oven to 350°F. Remove any fat or gristle from the meat. Cut the meat into medallions. Roll a strip of bacon around the sides of each medallion, and secure with kitchen string. Heat the olive oil in a skillet, and seal the medallions on all sides. Place the medallions in a roasting pan in the oven, and cook for about 20 minutes. Cooking time will depend on the thickness of the meat and individual taste.

Remove any excess oil from the skillet, leaving about 1 tablespoon, and slowly cook the shallot and carrot. Increase the heat; add the port and then the stock. Bring to a boil and let reduce by about a third. Pour the sauce into a blender or food processor and purée, adding three-quarters of the pitted prunes, a few at a time. Season to taste, and reheat the sauce. Serve the medallions on the sauce, and garnish with the remaining whole prunes.

HAM WITH LENTILS
PETIT SALÉ AUX LENTILLES

This is a real country dish. The French name "petit salé" actually means small and salty. Be careful with the seasoning – remember the ham will be quite salty. I sometimes add a few spoonfuls of mustard to this dish.

Serves 6

INGREDIENTS
2½ pounds boneless ham
6 small herb sausages
2 pounds green lentils
1 large onion, stuck with 2 whole
  cloves
8 ounces carrots, cut into chunks
Bouquet garni
Salt and freshly ground black
  pepper

Wash the ham under running water. Put it into a large saucepan, and cover with cold water. Bring to a boil; reduce the heat, and simmer for 2 hours. After 2 hours, add the sausages to the saucepan, and cook for an additional 10 minutes. Remove the pan from the heat.

Cook the lentils in a large quantity of water with the onion, carrot, bouquet garni and a little salt. Bring them slowly to a boil; reduce the heat, and simmer for 30-40 minutes. Do not boil too rapidly, or the lentils will disintegrate. After about 30 minutes, add the ham and the sausages, and continue cooking until the lentils are tender. Drain off a little liquid, if necessary, and remove the bouquet garni. Cut the meat and the sausages into chunks. Put back into the saucepan to reheat, and serve.

ROAST PORK WITH GARLIC CREAM

This creamy sauce, well flavored with garlic, makes a marvelous accompaniment to lean roast pork. Brown the pork well before transferring it to the oven to finish cooking.

Serves 6

INGREDIENTS

2¼ pounds boneless pork loin
2 tablespoons olive oil
1 whole head garlic, all the
   cloves peeled
Scant ½ cup port
1¼ cups heavy cream, whipped
Salt and freshly ground black
   pepper
Knob of butter

Preheat the oven to 400°F. Trim any excess fat or gristle from the meat, setting the trimmings aside for use in the sauce. Roll the meat into a roast, and secure it with string. Sauté the meat trimmings in half the oil with the garlic, and let brown slightly. Pour off any excess fat from the pan, and stir in the port. Remove from the heat, and stir in the cream. Remove a few cloves of garlic for garnish. Purée the sauce until smooth in a blender, and then press it through a fine strainer into a clean pan. Return the sauce to the heat, and let it reduce a little. Remove from the heat.

Heat the remaining oil and the butter in a large skillet, and seal the pork on all sides. Transfer it to a roasting pan, and cook in the oven for 20-40 minutes, depending on the thickness of the roast. Reheat the sauce slowly. Slice the pork, and serve with the sauce poured over and the few cloves of garlic as garnish.

PROVENÇAL PORK

I always feel that there aren't sufficient casserole recipes for pork – but, of course, the French have plenty! The pork is flavored with tomatoes and herbs, and topped with sliced potatoes.

Serves 6

INGREDIENTS

2¼ pounds pork tenderloins
¼ cup butter
3 cups thinly sliced onions
14-ounce can tomatoes
Salt and freshly ground black
   pepper
1 tablespoon freshly chopped
   mixed herbs
1½ pounds potatoes, thinly sliced
1 tablespoon freshly chopped
   parsley

Preheat the oven to 350°F. Trim the pork of any surplus fat, and slice it thinly. Melt half the butter in a large skillet, and slowly fry the slices of meat, stirring continuously to prevent them from burning. Transfer the meat to a plate, and set aside. Stir the onions into the meat juices in the skillet, and cook slowly until just soft. Add the tomatoes to the pan along with the salt, pepper and mixed herbs. Bring to a boil, then simmer slowly for 5 minutes, or until the sauce has reduced by about a third.

Arrange the meat, sauce and potatoes in layers in an ovenproof serving dish, finishing with a layer of potato. Melt the remaining butter, and brush it over the top layer of potato. Cover the dish with a lid or foil, and cook in the oven for 1½ hours. Remove the lid or foil, and cook for an additional 30 minutes to brown the potatoes. Sprinkle with chopped parsley before serving.

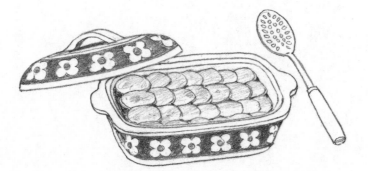

CASSOULET

Cassoulet has almost as many recipes as I've had hot dinners! The main ingredient is navy beans, and it should include a mixture of meats. I often place a layer of bread crumbs over my cassoulet, and brown them, uncovered, in the oven.

Serves 6–8

INGREDIENTS
1 pound navy beans, presoaked
    for 12 hours
¼ cup goose or other poultry
    drippings
1 pork knuckle
1 pound pork loin
1 onion, sliced
2 cloves garlic, chopped
1 leek, cut into chunks
4 tomatoes, halved
1 carrot, cut into chunks
1 bay leaf
Bouquet garni
8 ounces herb or garlic sausages
12 ounces bacon, in one piece
½ lamb shoulder
Salt and freshly ground black
    pepper

Drain and rinse the navy beans. Melt the drippings in a large flameproof casserole, and fry the pork knuckle and the loin to seal. Then add the onion, garlic, leek, tomatoes, carrot, bay leaf and bouquet garni. Stir well and cook for a few minutes. Add the drained beans, and enough water to cover the contents of the casserole. Bring to a boil, then reduce the heat. Cover the pan, and simmer slowly for 2 hours. After about 1 hour, add the sausages, bacon and lamb shoulder. Check the water level during cooking, and add water when necessary. After the full 2 hours, strain off the juice into a clean saucepan, and chop the meat into small pieces. Discard most of the bones. Remove the bay leaf and the bouquet garni.

Preheat the oven to 375°F. Layer the chopped meats, beans and sausage in the casserole. Add 2½-3 cups of the cooking liquor. Cover the casserole, and cook in the oven for 35 minutes. Serve piping hot from the oven.

LAMB IN RED WINE
SAUTÉ D'AGNEAU

This is a quick and easy recipe to cook. The rich mushroom sauce is very special. I like to serve this with buttered noodles.

Serves 4

INGREDIENTS
2 tablespoons olive oil
2¼ pounds boneless and cubed lamb shoulder
3 stalks celery, sliced
1 onion, finely chopped
8 ounces mushrooms
¾ cup red wine
¾ cup beef stock
1 tablespoon tomato paste
2 tablespoons cornstarch mixed with 2 tablespoons water
Salt and freshly ground black pepper

Warm half the olive oil in a skillet, and seal the pieces of lamb on all sides. Let brown slightly; then remove the lamb from the pan with a draining spoon, and keep it warm. Add the remaining oil, and sauté the celery, onion and mushrooms until softened. Add the wine, stock, tomato paste and the dissolved cornstarch. Stir until the sauce boils and thickens, heating slowly. Return the lamb to the skillet with the sauce, and add a little salt and pepper. Cover the pan, and cook for an additional 15-25 minutes. Remove the lamb, and purée the sauce in a blender until smooth. Serve the meat with the sauce poured over.

FILLET OF LAMB WITH FRESH THYME SAUCE

Lamb is very popular in France. Especially at the start of the season, it is served very pink in the center – you may need to roast the lamb for about 45 minutes if you prefer it well done. This recipe is a celebration of spring lamb.

Serves 6

INGREDIENTS
½ cup olive oil
1 rack of lamb, boneless but kept whole (reserve bones for the sauce)
1 carrot, finely chopped
1 onion, finely chopped
½ cup dry white wine
4 sprigs fresh thyme
⅔ cup butter
Salt and freshly ground black pepper

Preheat the oven to 400°F. Heat half the olive oil in a large pan, and sauté the lamb bones with the carrot and onion. Drain off any excess fat; then add the wine, and heat until almost evaporated, stirring continuously. Cover the ingredients with water, and cook at a slow boil, uncovered, for 1 hour. Drain the juices through a very fine strainer into a clean saucepan. Cook over a high heat, with the thyme, and let reduce until quite thick.

Heat 2 tablespoons of the butter and the remaining oil in the skillet, and seal the lamb on all sides. Transfer it to a roasting pan, and finish cooking the lamb in the oven for 15 minutes. Just before serving, drain the reduced juices through a fine strainer to remove the thyme. Mix the remaining butter into the sauce, a little at a time, and blend until smooth with a hand mixer or whisk. Cut the lamb into slices, and serve with the sauce.

FILLET OF LAMB IN PASTRY
FILET D'AGNEAU EN CROÛTE

"En croûte" means wrapped in pastry. Beef fillet is often cooked in this way, and is a real treat – lamb tenderloin is also delicious and much more affordable!

Serves 6

INGREDIENTS
2 lamb fillets, cut from the neck
  or the loin
Salt and freshly ground black
  pepper
1 tablespoon olive oil
⅓ cup butter
1 carrot, finely chopped
1 onion, finely chopped
1 sprig thyme
1 bay leaf
1¼ cups white wine
8 ounces prepared puff pastry
1 clove garlic, chopped
2 tablespoons freshly chopped
  parsley
1 egg, beaten

Preheat the oven to 425°F. Prepare the lamb fillets, removing and retaining any fat or gristle for the sauce. Lightly pepper the meat. Warm the oil and a knob of butter in a skillet, and seal the meat on all sides. Remove the meat with a draining spoon, and keep warm. Sauté the lamb trimmings, carrot, onion, thyme and bay leaf in the pan. Wipe off the excess fat, and add the white wine to the pan. Boil until almost evaporated, scraping up any meat sediment. Cover the vegetables with water, and bring to a boil; then skim off any fat which rises to the surface, and reduce and thicken.

Roll out the dough very thinly and cut into 2 rectangles. Place the fillets on the dough, and sprinkle with the chopped garlic and parsley. Fold the dough round the fillets. Seal the edges with the beaten egg, and brush a little egg over the top. Bake for about 15 minutes, until the pastry is browned and crisp. Press the thickened sauce through a fine strainer, and return it to the heat in a clean saucepan. Let it reduce a little and thicken. Stir in the remaining butter. Cut the encased fillet into slices, and serve with the sauce.

PROVENÇAL LAMB

Use red or white wine in this Mediterranean-style lamb casserole. I actually think that white wine produces a better flavor for lamb when it is cooked in this way, but make sure that you use a dry white wine.

Serves 4

INGREDIENTS

1 pound lamb from a cooked leg
¼ cup butter
1 tablespoon olive oil
2 medium onions, chopped
1 clove garlic, crushed
14-ounce can tomatoes
1 tablespoon tomato paste
1¼ cups dry white wine
1⅓ cups sliced mushrooms
1 large green bell pepper, seeded and sliced
Salt and freshly ground black pepper

Cut the lamb into small dice. Heat the butter with the olive oil. Add the onions and garlic, and cook over a low heat for 10-15 minutes until softened but not browned. Stir in the tomatoes, tomato paste and wine, and bring to a boil. Add the lamb. Cover the pan, and simmer for 25 minutes. Add the mushrooms and green bell pepper, and cook for an additional 15 minutes, stirring occasionally. Season to taste, and serve.

LAMB WITH SPRING VEGETABLES

NAVARIN PRINTANIER

This stew is traditionally made with mutton, although such dishes are now usually made with lamb.

Serves 6

INGREDIENTS
6 tablespoons vegetable oil
12 lamb chops, trimmed
Flour mixed with salt, pepper and pinch of dried thyme
2 shallots, finely chopped
1 clove garlic, crushed
2½ cups brown stock
⅔ cup dry white wine
5 tomatoes, skinned, seeded and roughly chopped
Bouquet garni

Spring Vegetables
12 new potatoes, scrubbed but not peeled
8 baby carrots, scraped (if green tops are in good condition, leave them on)
6 small turnips, peeled and left whole
8 ounces thin green beans, cut into 1-inch lengths on the diagonal
2 cups frozen petits pois
12 scallions, root ends and green tops trimmed, about 3 inches in length
1 tablespoon freshly chopped parsley (optional)

Preheat the oven to 350°F. Heat about half the oil in a large, heavy-based skillet. Dredge the lamb chops with the flour mixture, shaking off any excess.

Brown the chops four at a time, adding more oil if necessary. When the chops are brown on all sides, transfer them to a heavy flameproof casserole. Drain most of the oil from the pan. Add the shallots and garlic, and cook over a medium heat, stirring continuously. Add the stock and wine, and bring to a boil, scraping the bottom of the pan to remove the browned meat juices. Let boil rapidly to reduce slightly, then add the tomatoes. Pour the sauce over the lamb, turning the chops to coat them with the sauce. Add the bouquet garni. Cover the casserole tightly, and cook in the oven for about 30 minutes, or until the lamb is tender.

After about 10 minutes, add the potatoes and carrots to the lamb. Add the turnips, green beans, peas and scallions 15 minutes before the end of the cooking time. After 30 minutes, remove the lamb and any vegetables that are tender to a warmed serving dish. Boil the sauce rapidly to reduce it and to cook any vegetables that need extra time. Pour the sauce over the lamb and vegetables, and sprinkle with chopped parsley, if wished.

BOURGUIGNON BEEF

A classic dish from Burgundy, so choose a good red wine of that region for cooking. Long, slow cooking and prime ingredients are the real secrets of success!

Serves 6-8

INGREDIENTS

6 slices smoked bacon, cut into small pieces
20 baby onions, peeled
1 tablespoon olive oil
4½ pounds braising steak, cut into cubes
2 tablespoons all-purpose flour
1 bottle red wine
Salt and freshly ground black pepper

In a large saucepan cook the bacon and the onions without adding any extra fat. Remove them with a draining spoon when they begin to brown. Add the oil and the meat, and cook quickly to brown and seal the meat on all sides. Sprinkle with the flour, and let it brown slightly; then add the wine, stirring well. Add water to cover only if necessary. Add salt and pepper and bring to a boil. Reduce the heat, and return the onions and bacon to the pan. Cover the pan, and simmer very slowly for 3 hours, or until the beef is tender. Season and serve hot.

TOURNEDOS STEAKS WITH HERB BUTTER TOURNEDOS MAÎTRE D'HÔTEL

Tournedos steaks are cut from the very best end of the fillet. They are a real treat and should, I think, be cooked simply. In this recipe they are served with a herb butter – "maître d'hôtel."

Serves 6

INGREDIENTS
½ cup butter, softened at room temperature
2 tablespoons freshly chopped herbs
1 teaspoon lemon juice
Salt and freshly ground black pepper
6 tournedos steaks

Beat the butter in a bowl until quite soft. Add the herbs, and beat well; then add the lemon juice and a little salt and pepper. Put the butter on a sheet of foil, and form it into a roll. Put the butter into the freezer to harden.

Cook the steaks under a hot broiler to your own preference, and serve on a warmed dish topped with the cold butter cut into slices – one slice on each steak.

HUNTER'S TOURNEDOS STEAKS

This rich mushroom sauce, a classic used in many French dishes, may be served over any steaks, chicken pieces or pork fillet. Use white wine if you prefer, but I like red best!

Serves 6

INGREDIENTS
¼ cup butter
2½ cups sliced mushrooms
1 tablespoon freshly chopped
  tarragon
½ cup chopped shallots
3 tablespoons Cognac
½ cup red wine
1 cup beef stock
Salt and freshly ground black
  pepper
6 tournedos steaks

Melt 1½ tablespoons of the butter in a skillet, and cook the mushrooms, tarragon and shallots until tender. Add the Cognac, and cook until almost evaporated. Stir in the wine and the stock, and season well. Let the sauce reduce until quite thick and syrupy.

Cook the steaks under a hot broiler to your own preference. Whisk the remaining butter into the sauce, and serve it poured over the steaks.

WHITE VEAL STEW
BLANQUETTE DE VEAU

A white stew is known as a "blanquette," and is usually made with white meat – veal, pork or chicken. Chicken is the best alternative to veal for this recipe. Garnish with chopped parsley or watercress.

Serves 4

INGREDIENTS
2½ cups diced boneless veal
2 onions, chopped
1 leek, chopped
2 carrots, chopped
Salt and white pepper
2 tablespoons butter
2 tablespoons all-purpose flour
2 cups sliced button mushrooms
1 egg yolk, beaten
Scant 1 cup milk
Scant 1 cup light cream

Put the cubes of meat in a large flameproof casserole. Cover with cold water, and bring to a boil. Add the onions, leek, carrots, salt and pepper. Return to a boil; then reduce the heat, and cover the casserole. Cook until the meat is tender, skimming off the fat that rises to the surface occasionally – this will take about 1 hour. Remove the cooked meat with a draining spoon, and keep it warm.

Melt the butter, and stir in the flour. Gradually add the cooking liquor from the casserole, stirring continuously, and heat until the sauce boils and thickens. Add the mushrooms. Reduce the heat, and cook for 15 minutes, stirring regularly. Beat the milk and cream into the egg yolk, and beat half of this mixture into the sauce. When it is well incorporated, beat in the remaining mixture, beating continuously to avoid curdling. Do not allow the sauce to boil. Add the sauce to the meat; reheat and serve in a warmed serving dish.

SIRLOIN STEAK WITH CIDER SAUCE

A dish from Normandy featuring apples and cider but, surprisingly, no cream! Carve the steak into slices at the table if you prefer – it looks impressive!

Serves 4

INGREDIENTS
⅓ cup butter
2 tablespoons oil
1 shallot, chopped
1 apple, peeled, cored and sliced
2½ cups dry cider
1¼ cups beef stock
1 piece sirloin steak, weighing about 2¼ pounds

Heat 1 tablespoon of the butter in a skillet with the oil. Add the shallot and apple slices, and cook until tender. Add the cider, increase the heat, and let the juices reduce. Stir in the stock and allow the sauce to reduce once again – but not too much as the apples will make the sauce quite thick. Press the contents of the pan through a fine strainer then purée in a blender or food processor until smooth.

Cook the steak in a skillet, to your own preference then carve it into slices. Arrange on a warmed serving dish. Reheat the sauce, and whisk in the remaining butter before serving.

STEAK IN GREEN PEPPERCORN SAUCE STEAK AU POIVRE

Green peppercorns are pretty hot, so reduce the quantity used in this recipe if you are cautious by nature!

Serves 4

INGREDIENTS
½ cup green peppercorns in brine
2 tablespoons Dijon mustard
4 fillet steaks
4 tablespoons butter
1 cup heavy cream
½ teaspoon salt
1 tablespoon freshly chopped parsley

Drain the peppercorns, and rinse them. Pat dry on paper towels, and crush them in a pestle and mortar or in a small bowl, using the end of a rolling pin. Mix the crushed peppercorns with the mustard, and spread this on both sides of the steaks. Melt the butter in a large, heavy-bottomed skillet over a high heat. When the foam subsides, add the steaks, and fry for 2 minutes on each side. This will produce rare steaks. Double the time for medium–rare, and allow about 12 minutes for well-done steaks. Transfer the steaks from the pan to a serving dish, and keep them warm while you finish the sauce.

Add the cream and salt to the pan, and cook over a low heat for a few minutes, scraping all the sediment from the bottom of the pan and incorporating it in the sauce.

Remove the pan from the heat, and pour the sauce over the steaks. Sprinkle with parsley, and serve at once.

BEEF IN BEER CARBONNADE À LA FLAMANDE

Cooking beef in beer makes a dish known as a "Carbonnade." These are more common in the north of France, toward the Flemish border, where more "dark beer," brown ale or bitter, is drunk. I sometimes spoon a little crème fraîche into a Carbonnade before serving.

Serves 6

INGREDIENTS
2 tablespoons oil
1½ pounds braising steak
1 large onion, thinly sliced
¼ cup all-purpose flour
1 clove garlic, crushed
1¼ cups brown ale
1¼ cups hot water
Bouquet garni
Salt and freshly ground black
  pepper
Pinch of sugar
Nutmeg
Dash of red wine vinegar
Dijon mustard
6 slices French bread cut about
  ½ inch thick

Preheat the oven to 325°F. Heat the oil in a large, heavy-bottomed skillet. Cut the meat into 2-inch pieces, and brown quickly on both sides in the oil. Brown 5-6 pieces at a time to avoid crowding the pan.

Transfer the meat from the pan to a casserole when browned. Reduce the heat, and add the onion to the pan. Cook until the onion is beginning to soften and color, then stir in the flour, and add the garlic. Cook for about 1 minute. Add the ale, hot water, bouquet garni, salt and pepper, with a little sugar, nutmeg and vinegar. Bring to a boil then transfer to the casserole with the meat. Cover the casserole, and cook in the oven for 2-2½ hours.

Fifteen minutes before serving, skim off any fat from the surface, and reserve it. Spread the mustard on the bread, and spoon some of the fat over each slice.

Place the bread on top of the casserole, pushing it down slightly. Cook for an additional 15-20 minutes, uncovered, or until the bread is browned and crisp.

BOEUF EN DAUBE

As with so many classic dishes, there are countless recipes for daube – a rich beef stew originally cooked in a daubière, an earthenware cooking pot. I often add a little orange rind and lots of thyme to the basic recipe.

Serves 6

INGREDIENTS

2¼ pounds chuck steak
8 ounces diced smoked bacon
4 sprigs parsley
4 cloves garlic, chopped
Salt and freshly ground black
    pepper
2 tablespoons olive oil
2 onions, chopped
2 carrots, chopped
1 bottle red wine

Remove any excess fat from the meat, and cut into quite large cubes. Slice the cubes open on one side, and put a little bacon, parsley, garlic, salt and pepper in each. Close each cube of meat, and secure with a toothpick. Heat the olive oil in a skillet, and seal the meat on all sides. Remove the toothpicks. Empty the contents of the pan into a flameproof casserole, and add the onion, carrot and wine. Bring to a boil and let the liquid reduce a little. Cover the pan, and cook over a low heat for 3 hours. Check the level of the juices from time to time; stir, and add water if necessary. Season to taste, and serve.

BEEF WITH OLIVES
ESTOUFFADE DE BOEUF

A rich beef casserole, similar to a daube, but with the flavorings of Provence – olives, thyme and mushrooms. This is one of my favorite dishes!

Serves 6

INGREDIENTS

2 tablespoons olive oil
8 ounces diced smoked bacon
2¼ pounds best braising steak, cut into small pieces
2 tablespoons all-purpose flour
4 onions, sliced
Salt and freshly ground black pepper
1 bottle dry red wine
Bouquet garni (with lots of thyme)
2 cloves garlic, chopped
2 cups sliced mushrooms
1 cup pitted black olives

Preheat the oven to 325°F. Heat 1 tablespoon of the olive oil in a large, flameproof casserole, and cook the bacon until the juices run. Toss the steak in the flour, and shake off any excess. Add to the casserole with the bacon and onions, and brown the meat on all sides. Drain off any excess fat.

Add salt and pepper, and the wine. Stir well, then let the wine reduce over a high heat, until about half of the liquid remains. Add the bouquet garni and garlic. Cover the casserole, and cook in the oven for 2 hours, checking and stirring occasionally.

Sauté the mushrooms in the remaining olive oil. Drain the contents of the casserole through a large strainer, catching the juices in a clean saucepan. Put the meat and onions back into the casserole, and add the sautéed mushrooms. Return the juices to the heat; skim off any rising fat, and stir in the olives. Pour this sauce back over the contents of the casserole, and cook in the oven or on the stove top for an additional 20 minutes. Remove the bouquet garni, and season to taste. Serve hot.

NORMANDY VEAL WITH APPLES AND CALVADOS

Most supermarkets now sell turkey escalopes, which could be used in place of veal in this traditional dish from Normandy. Do not overcook the meat – it needs a very short cooking time.

Serves 4

INGREDIENTS
2 eating apples
½ cup butter
⅔ cup thinly sliced mushrooms
4 4-ounce veal escalopes, beaten thin
Salt and freshly ground black pepper
4 tablespoons Calvados
⅔ cup heavy cream or thick yogurt
2 tablespoons lemon juice
1 tablespoon freshly chopped chives or parsley

Peel, core and thinly slice the apples. Melt the butter in a large skillet. When it starts to foam, add the apple and mushroom slices, and fry slowly until tender and just starting to brown. Remove the apples and mushrooms, and set aside. Season the escalopes with salt and pepper. Add to the pan, and fry quickly on both sides.

Warm the Calvados in a small saucepan; set it alight, and pour it over the veal. Carefully move the skillet so the liqueur is evenly distributed, until the flames die down. Reduce the heat, and add the cream or yogurt, lemon juice, apples and mushrooms. Cook for an additional 2-3 minutes, stirring continuously until the sauce starts to thicken. Do not boil. Transfer the escalopes to a warmed serving dish. Adjust the seasoning of the sauce if necessary, and pour over the meat. Garnish with the chives or parsley.

KIDNEYS WITH DIJON MUSTARD

This is my favorite way of serving kidneys! Use a smooth Dijon mustard for this smooth, rich sauce. I serve the kidneys with rice or pasta, and then follow it up with a tossed green salad.

Serves 6

INGREDIENTS
1½ pounds lamb's kidneys
¼ cup unsalted butter
1-2 shallots, finely chopped
1¼ cups dry white wine
⅓ cup lightly salted butter, softened
3 tablespoons Dijon mustard
Salt, freshly ground black pepper and lemon juice, to taste
2 tablespoons freshly chopped parsley

Trim away any fat from the kidneys, and slice them in half lengthwise. Carefully snip out any hard core from the center using a pair of sharp scissors. Melt the unsalted butter in a large skillet, and fry the kidneys, uncovered, slowly over a low heat until they are lightly browned on all sides. Remove the kidneys from the skillet with a draining spoon, and keep them warm.

Add the shallots to the meat juices in the pan, and cook for about 1 minute, stirring frequently, until they are just soft. Add the wine, and bring to a boil, stirring continuously and scraping the bottom of the pan to remove any browned juices. Boil the sauce rapidly for 3-4 minutes to reduce it by about half. Remove the pan from the heat. Add the softened butter to the pan with the mustard and seasonings. Whisk the mixture into the reduced sauce with a small whisk or fork. Return the pan to the heat, and add the kidneys and the parsley. Heat very slowly for 1-2 minutes, taking care not to boil the mixture any further. Serve immediately.

KIDNEYS TURBIGO

Always use freshly ground black pepper in this dish to achieve a spicy flavor. The sauce is rich, and the dish needs little more than creamy mashed potatoes served with it.

Serves 4-6

Ingredients
8 lamb's kidneys
6 chipolata sausages
12 pearl onions
¼ cup butter
¼ cup all-purpose flour
2 cups stock – beef or chicken
⅔ cup dry white wine
2 teaspoons tomato paste
3 tablespoons dry or medium dry sherry
Salt and freshly ground black pepper
1 bay leaf
Croûtons and parsley to garnish

Cut the kidneys in half, removing the white core and any skin, and also cut the sausages. Melt the butter in a large, heavy-bottomed pan, and fry the kidneys and sausages until they are well browned. Remove from the pan, and keep hot.

Peel the pearl onions, leaving them whole, and put them into a pan of cold water. Bring to a boil and let simmer for 5 minutes, then drain. Set aside.

Stir the flour into the pan containing the butter and meat juices, and cook for 2-3 minutes. Gradually add the stock and wine, stirring continuously until the sauce is thickened and smooth. Bring to a boil, and blend in the tomato paste and sherry. Season to taste. Return the kidneys and sausages to the pan, together with the drained onions and the bay leaf. Cover with a lid, and simmer gently for about 25 minutes.

Remove the bay leaf, and transfer the kidney mixture to a serving dish. Garnish with croûtons and chopped parsley.

CALF'S LIVER WITH ORANGE SAUCE

Liver and kidneys are very popular in France – I love them too! Liver is usually cooked very quickly, so that it is browned on the outside and pink in the middle. Cook it a little more if you like, but do not overcook and toughen it.

Serves 6

INGREDIENTS
⅓ cup butter
1 large piece of calf's liver about 1½-2 pounds, cut into slices
4 oranges (2 squeezed for their juice, and the remaining 2 peeled of skin and pith and cut into thin slices)
1¼ cups veal or chicken stock
Salt and freshly ground black pepper
1 tablespoon freshly chopped chives to garnish

Melt most of the butter in a large skillet, and cook the liver briskly until browned on both sides. Remove the liver, and keep it warm on a plate over a saucepan of boiling water. Wipe the pan to remove any excess fat. Add the juice of 2 of the oranges, and cook rapidly, scraping the bottom of the pan with a wooden spoon to mix any remaining liver sediment into the juice. Add the veal stock, salt and pepper. Bring to a boil, and add the orange slices. Let the orange color slightly; then remove the slices with a fork, and place them on the liver.

Remove the pan from the heat, and stir in the remaining butter. Season to taste. Serve the sauce poured over the liver and sliced oranges, and garnish with the chopped chives.

STEAMED CALF'S LIVER

Another simple but rich recipe for liver. Steam the liver quite briskly – or you could slice the liver and pan-fry or broil it if preferred. I think the liver is more attractive with a browned exterior!

Serves 4

INGREDIENTS
1 sprig fresh tarragon
6 tablespoons wine vinegar
2 shallots, chopped
1 teaspoon peppercorns, lightly crushed
1¼ cups whipping cream, whipped
⅓ cup milk
2¼ pounds whole calf's liver, trimmed and skin removed
Salt and freshly ground black pepper
¼ cup butter

Chop half the tarragon finely, and put it into a saucepan with the vinegar, shallots and peppercorns. Heat, and let boil until the vinegar has almost completely evaporated, then whisk in the cream and the milk. Let reduce slightly, then press the sauce through a fine strainer. Remove from the heat, and keep warm.

Steam the whole liver on a bed of the remaining tarragon until still just pink in the center: this will take 10-15 minutes. Season with salt and pepper. Slice the liver thinly, and place on a heated serving dish. Put the sauce back over a low heat, and whisk in the butter. Season and serve immediately.

KIDNEY FRICASSÉE

Sautéed veal kidneys in a sweet, creamy sauce. Lamb's kidneys may be easier to obtain than veal kidneys, and they work just as well in this recipe. If any blood runs from the kidneys, drain it away and do not add it to the sauce. Serve with rice.

Serves 6

Ingredients
2 pounds veal or lamb's kidneys
1 tablespoon olive oil
3 cups sliced mushrooms
Salt and white pepper
2 tablespoons Madeira
Scant 1 cup veal stock
6 tablespoons heavy cream

Prepare the kidneys by cutting into small cubes, removing the cores. Heat the oil in a skillet and sauté the kidney and the mushrooms until cooked to your liking. Season with salt and pepper. Remove the kidneys, and keep warm. Deglaze the skillet with the Madeira, letting it almost evaporate; then stir in the stock, and reduce by half. Add the cream, and salt and pepper to taste. Return the kidneys to the sauce to reheat. Serve hot.

VEGETABLES

In common with most cooks, I just love being in France and shopping in the French markets. The range of fruits and vegetables is absolutely astounding, all displayed in top condition. It is impossible for me to spend even a few hours on French soil without buying at least 2 pounds of endive and half a dozen Breton artichokes!

Vegetables and salads are seldom eaten with the main course in France, but are enjoyed separately, between the main course and the dessert. This allows the vegetables to be savored in their own right, rather than merely served as an accompaniment to fill up the plate!

Seasonal Variety

Modern supermarkets have certainly helped in the shrinking of our ever-diminishing world, but they have also offered us the benefit of a huge array of produce from many lands, available all year. What makes the French style of vegetable cookery so different is that most people prefer to shop in markets, where they are offered and buy the best of what is in season. How often do you actually notice a basket of fresh walnuts in your supermarket in October? In a French market you cannot but be aware of the huge displays of nuts, and so you know that, at that moment, there is something special about walnuts. Oh, for such reliability elswhere! I find that my local market will sell almost the same range of produce as the supermarket in an attempt to compete, rather than concentrating on what is fresh and best.

Garlic – a Taste of France

There are several vegetables without which it is impossible even to contemplate the preparation of a French meal! The first of these must surely be garlic. The most important thing to remember is that the fresher the garlic, the milder its flavor. The huge bulbs of very juicy garlic available in late summer and early fall have a flavor that is less likely to remain with you to the following day than the smaller, drier cloves you might buy and use in the spring! Also remember that the redder the skin of the garlic, the stronger the flavor – it is almost like a social acceptability warning system! Cooked garlic is less pungent than raw (it's the practise of using garlic in butter and salad dressings that will make you unpopular with non-garlic eaters!), and dried garlic, garlic granules or garlic salt bear no relation to the real thing!

Artichokes – my Favorite Vegetable

Globe artichokes, as I have already mentioned, are one of the vegetables that I always seek out when I am in France. I am certain that many people are deterred from eating some of the slightly more exotic vegetables, such as artichokes, simply because they are not certain how to prepare them. I think that artichokes are one of the most romantic of foods – one will generally serve two people, so there is an intimacy in the eating, and they take some time to consume, letting you relax and enjoy a glass of wine. I generally serve an artichoke as an appetizer. Trim the stalk close to the globe, and snip off the tops of the leaves, especially if they are spiky and non-finger friendly! Boil the artichoke for about 40 minutes, according to size, until dark green in color. The outer leaves will pull off easily when the artichoke is ready.

A License to Flirt!

Serve the artichoke with vinaigrette, garlic mayonnaise or melted butter. Take off the leaves, and dip the bases, drawing them through your teeth to remove the fleshy part. It will take you some time to work your way through to the center, the hairy choke. Remove this with a teaspoon, and divide the remaining fleshy heart, the *fond*, between the diners. This is the *pièce de la résistance* of the artichoke, and should be liberally coated in the remaining dressing or butter before eating! Delicious! Of course, the French for "flirt" is *fond d'artichaut!* As a respectable married woman, I must point out that this is not why I am so addicted to the vegetable . . .

The other vegetable that I have really appreciated since first traveling to France is chicory, more commonly known as endive. Even now I am not keen on raw endive, which is often served in salads with orange, as it has a very bitter taste. Roasted in a hot oven with a little finely chopped onion, salt, pepper and olive oil it is quite different and utterly delicious!

FENNEL RAMEKINS

These light fennel molds are easy to prepare and cook, and, with their aniseed flavor, make an original dish. Be sure that the fennel is well cooked, and that you have exactly 2½ cups of the purée.

Serves 6

INGREDIENTS

2 pounds fennel bulbs, cut into quarters
5 cups milk
4 eggs, beaten
1 tablespoon Pernod, or other aniseed alcohol
Scant 1 cup heavy cream
Salt and freshly ground black pepper
A little butter for greasing

Preheat the oven to 325°F. Cut away any hard patches from the fennel, and discard them. Poach the fennel in the milk for about 30 minutes, then leave to drain well. When the fennel is well drained, put the quarters into a blender or food processor, and blend until smooth – this should make about 2½ cups of pulp. If necessary, make up to the required amount by adding some of the cooking milk. Whisk in the eggs, Pernod, cream, salt and pepper.

Butter 6 ramekin dishes, and fill them three-quarters full with the fennel mixture. Place the ramekins in a high-sided dish, and add water to come halfway up the sides of the ramekins. Cook in the oven for 30-40 minutes. To serve, invert the ramekins onto warmed serving plates.

STUFFED ARTICHOKE HEARTS

When artichokes are at the height of their season and relatively cheap, they make a most exotic vegetable to stuff. Cut away most of the leaves, and boil the artichokes for 20–30 minutes. Canned artichokes are convenient, but a poor substitute for fresh.

Serves 6

INGREDIENTS

6 large fresh or canned globe
    artichoke hearts
Juice of 1 lemon
2½ cups finely chopped
    mushrooms
Knob of butter
¾ cup finely chopped ham
¾ cup chopped *Jambon de
    Bayonne*, or similar smoked
    ham
Salt and freshly ground black
    pepper
1 cup grated cheese

Sauce
2 tablespoons butter
¼ cup flour
1¼ cups milk
Pinch of nutmeg
Salt and freshly ground black
    pepper
3 tablespoons light cream

Preheat the oven to 400°F. Cook the fresh artichoke hearts in boiling water with half the lemon juice, until tender. Drain well, and remove the hairy "choke." Coat the hearts with the remaining lemon juice, and set aside. Cook the mushrooms with the knob of butter over a high heat for a few minutes, until their juices run. Remove from the heat, and discard the juices. Stir the chopped hams, salt and pepper into the mushrooms, and heat thoroughly .

To make the sauce, melt the butter in a saucepan; beat in the flour, and cook for 1 minute. Gradually add the milk, and beat continuously until the mixture boils and thickens. Reduce the heat, and cook for an additional 2 minutes. Remove from the heat, and stir in the nutmeg, salt, pepper and cream.

Stir most of the cheese into the ham and mushroom mixture. Pile this mixture onto the artichoke hearts. Grease an ovenproof dish. Place the prepared artichokes in it, and spoon the sauce over each artichoke. Scatter with the remaining grated cheese. Cook in the oven for 10-15 minutes, until well browned on the top.

ARTICHOKES WITH GARLIC MAYONNAISE
ARTICHAUTS AÏOLI

This is one of my favorite ways of serving artichokes – so simple and so delicious! Garlic butter is a good alternative, but this rich garlic mayonnaise is best!

Serves 4

INGREDIENTS
4 medium globe artichokes
1 slice lemon
1 bay leaf
Pinch of salt

Sauce Aïoli
2 egg yolks
2 cloves garlic, crushed
Salt, freshly ground black pepper
   and lemon juice to taste
1¼ cups olive oil
Chervil leaves to garnish

To prepare the artichokes, break off the stems, and twist to remove any tough fibers. Trim the base, so that the artichokes will stand upright. Trim the points from all the leaves, and wash the artichokes well. Bring a large saucepan full of water to a boil with the slice of lemon and bay leaf. Add a pinch of salt, and, when the water is boiling, add the artichokes. Let cook for 25 minutes over a medium heat. While the artichokes are cooking, prepare the sauce.

Beat the egg yolks and garlic with a pinch of salt and pepper in a deep bowl or in a blender or food processor. Add the olive oil a few drops at a time while beating by hand, or in a thin, steady stream with the machine running. If preparing the sauce by hand, when half the oil has been added, the remainder may be added in a thin steady stream. Add a little lemon juice when the sauce becomes very thick. When all the oil has been added, adjust the seasoning, and add more lemon juice to taste.

When the artichokes are cooked, the bottom leaves will pull away easily. Remove them from the water with a draining spoon, and drain upside–down on paper towels or in a colander. Let cool slightly, and serve with the sauce aïoli. Garnish with chervil.

BAKERY-STYLE POTATOES
POMMES DE TERRE
BOULANGÈRE

These potatoes are well-known as Pommes de Terre Boulangère – baked by the baker! They go well with any meat dish, and are almost good enough to eat by themselves!

Serves 4-6

INGREDIENTS

2 pounds potatoes, thinly sliced
1 large onion, finely chopped
Salt and freshly ground black
   pepper
2 cups hot stock
¼ cup butter

Preheat the oven to 350°F. Generously butter a wide, shallow baking dish. Arrange a layer of potatoes in the bottom of the dish, then a little onion, salt and pepper. Continue until you have used all the ingredients, finishing with a layer of potatoes and seasoning.

Pour over the stock, and dot the surface with knobs of butter. Place the dish on the highest shelf of the oven, and bake for 45 minutes. The potatoes should be soft when pierced with a sharp knife or skewer, and the top should be golden-brown. They can be placed under a hot broiler, if necessary, for extra browning.

BAKED ZUCCHINI

*This is a very popular way of cooking vegetables and fish –
use a roux-thickened cheese sauce, or a cream and cheese
mixture as in this recipe.*

Serves 4

INGREDIENTS
1 pound zucchinis
½ teaspoon salt
⅔ cup water
1 egg, lightly beaten
⅔ cup heavy cream
2 tablespoons grated Gruyère
   cheese, (Cheddar is a good
   alternative)
Freshly ground black pepper
1 tablespoon butter

Preheat the oven to 400°F. Wipe
the zucchini, trim the ends and
cut them into ½-inch slices. Put
them into a saucepan with the
salt and water. Cook over a
medium heat until almost all the
water has evaporated.

Mix together the egg, cream and
1 tablespoon of the cheese in a
small bowl. Season with black
pepper.

Carefully place the zucchini in a
gratin dish or shallow ovenproof
dish. Pour the cream mixture
over, and top with the remaining
cheese. Dot with butter, and
bake for about 10 minutes, or
until just set and golden-brown.

SAUERKRAUT SALAD

This recipe clearly shows the German influence on the cooking of Alsace, the region from which the salad comes. Fresh sauerkraut has more texture than canned, so I prefer to use it when possible.

Serves 6

INGREDIENTS
5 tablespoons olive oil
2 tablespoons wine vinegar
1 teaspoon sugar
Freshly ground black pepper
1 teaspoon cinnamon
½ teaspoon salt
1½ pounds cooked, fresh
  sauerkraut, soaked for 2 hours
Juice of 1 lemon
1 red apple, diced
2 small onions, chopped
2 carrots, grated

Mix the oil, vinegar, sugar, pepper, cinnamon and salt together in a large salad bowl, until all the sugar and salt has dissolved. Wash the sauerkraut in cold water, and drain well. Remove any excess moisture with a dry dish cloth. Cut the dry sauerkraut into equal lengths. Pour the lemon juice over the apple, onions and carrot. Mix all the ingredients together in the salad bowl, tossing them in the dressing.

BUTTERED CABBAGE

I am always grateful for new ideas for cooking cabbage! The addition of bacon and onion makes a very special dish from a rather humble vegetable.

Serves 8

INGREDIENTS

3 pounds cabbage, shredded
½ cup goose or other poultry drippings or lard
8 ounces chopped smoked bacon
1 medium onion, chopped
½ cup butter
Salt and freshly ground black pepper

Blanch the cabbage in boiling salted water for 4-5 minutes. Drain well. Melt the drippings or lard in a large skillet. Add the bacon, onion and cabbage, and stir well. Cover the pan, and cook over a very low heat for 20 minutes; then stir in the butter, and cook for an additional 20 minutes, covered. Season to taste, and serve in a heated serving dish.

CARROTS WITH ONIONS & BACON

This is a rich and colorful dish of carrots. New season's carrots have a sweet flavor, and are the best for this dish. On the other hand, it is an excellent way of making dull old carrots a little more exciting.

Serves 6

INGREDIENTS

3 tablespoons goose or poultry drippings
3 pounds carrots, finely sliced into rounds
1 pound onions, finely sliced
Bouquet garni
2¼ cups diced smoked bacon
1 teaspoon sugar
½ teaspoon cinnamon
Salt and freshly ground black pepper

Slowly melt the goose or poultry drippings in a large, heavy-based skillet, then increase the heat, and sauté the carrots, onions and bouquet garni. Shake the pan occasionally to prevent the vegetables from sticking. When the vegetables begin to color, reduce the heat; cover the pan, and cook for 25-30 minutes.

Blanch the bacon in boiling water for 3 minutes; drain well, and add to the carrot mixture. Sprinkle with the sugar and cinnamon; cover the pan, and cook until very tender. Season with salt and pepper before serving.

POTATO PATTIES WITH ONIONS
POMMES DARPHIN AUX OIGNONS

These little potato patties could be baked in muffin pans or ramekins. Oil the pans well so that the patties will release easily for a good presentation.

Serves 4

INGREDIENTS
4 large potatoes
1 onion, finely chopped
1 tablespoon freshly chopped
   herbs
Salt and freshly ground black
   pepper

Preheat the oven to 400°F. Cut the potatoes into small matchsticks, either by hand or in a machine. Stir the onion and herbs into the potato.

Oil 4 small molds and divide the mixture evenly between them. Season each patty with salt and pepper. Bake for 15 minutes. Invert the patties onto a baking sheet, and brown the tops under a hot broiler if necessary.

BAKED EGGPLANTS

Eggplants cooked in olive oil always remind me of summer vacations and sunshine. Be certain to wash the eggplants thoroughly to remove all the salt, or the dish will be spoiled.

Serves 6

INGREDIENTS

4 medium-sized eggplants, sliced
Salt and freshly ground black
    pepper
6 tablespoons olive oil
2 cloves garlic
2¼ pounds tomatoes, seeded and
    sliced
1 bay leaf
Pinch of thyme
1 tablespoon freshly chopped
    parsley
1 cup grated cheese

Spread the eggplant slices on a plate, and sprinkle liberally with salt, or layer them with salt in a colander. Let sit for about 30 minutes, then rinse thoroughly, and dry on paper towels.

Preheat the oven to 400°F. Fry the eggplants in 4 tablespoons of the olive oil over a high heat, but take care not to let them burn. Remove the slices from the skillet, and drain on paper towels. Retain any oil left in the pan. Add the remaining olive oil, and cook the garlic cloves. Cook slowly so that they flavor the oil. Remove the garlic, and discard it. Add the tomatoes, bay leaf and thyme, and cook for 20 minutes. Remove the bay leaf.

Pour half the tomato mixture into the bottom of an ovenproof dish. Sprinkle over the parsley, and add a little salt and pepper. Lay the slices of eggplant over the tomatoes, followed by half of the cheese, then the remaining tomato mixture and finally the remaining cheese. Bake for 15-20 minutes, until well browned.

BAKED BROCCOLI

This broccoli "au gratin" uses a cheese sauce based on a roux. For cooking "au gratin" using a cream sauce see the recipe for Baked Zucchini.

Serves 6

INGREDIENTS
3 large heads broccoli, trimmed
2 tablespoons butter
¼ cup all-purpose flour
1¼ cups milk
4 tablespoons heavy cream
Pinch of nutmeg
Salt and freshly ground black
  pepper
½ cup grated cheese

Preheat the oven to 400°F. Cook the broccoli in boiling salted water until almost cooked but slightly crisp. Plunge the broccoli immediately into cold water to stop it from cooking any more, then drain well.

Make a white sauce by melting the butter in a saucepan and stirring in the flour; cook for 1 minute and then gradually add the milk. Stir until boiling and thickened. Remove the sauce from the heat, and stir in the cream, nutmeg, salt, pepper and half the cheese.

Chop the broccoli roughly with a sharp knife, and mix it with the sauce. Transfer to an ovenproof dish. Sprinkle with the remaining cheese, and bake until the top is crisp and brown – about 15 minutes.

POTATOES DAUPHINOIS

This is a luxurious way of cooking potatoes. Bake them slowly to start with, so that they soften and absorb the cream, and then crisp them in the oven at its highest setting.

Serves 4–6

INGREDIENTS
2 tablespoons butter
4½ pounds potatoes, sliced
2½ cups light cream
1 clove garlic, crushed
Salt and freshly ground black
    pepper
Pinch of nutmeg
1 cup grated cheese

Preheat the oven to 325°F. Grease an ovenproof dish with the butter, and fill with the sliced potatoes. Mix the cream with the garlic, salt, pepper and nutmeg; then pour the cream over the potato. Bake for 1½ hours, adding a little milk if the cream does not cover the potatoes.

Remove the potatoes from the oven. Set the oven to its highest temperature. Sprinkle the grated cheese over the potatoes and bake until crisp and golden-brown, about 15 minutes.

TURNIPS IN CREAM

Turnips are often undervalued, but I think they are delicious. I often serve them in a parsley sauce – this recipe produces a much more luxurious dish.

Serves 8

INGREDIENTS
2¼ pounds turnips
1½ cups diced smoked bacon
1¼ cups light cream
Salt and freshly ground black
  pepper
Pinch of nutmeg

Cut the turnips into small cubes, and blanch them for 2 minutes in lightly salted boiling water. Remove and drain well. Put the turnip, bacon, cream, salt, pepper and nutmeg in a large saucepan, and cook over a low heat until the turnip has absorbed quite a lot of the cream. Serve piping hot on small individual plates.

SPRING SALAD

This is a striking and spicy salad, an unusual flavor being added by the horseradish. Remember that preparing horseradish might make you cry!

Serves 6

INGREDIENTS

1 lettuce, washed and shredded
1 cucumber, sliced
1 horseradish root, washed and
  evenly sliced
3 tomatoes, seeded and sliced
12-ounce can tuna fish, drained
12 black olives, pitted
6 scallions
A few sprigs of fresh mint
Scant 1 cup olive oil
3 drops Tabasco
6 tablespoons wine vinegar
Salt and freshly ground black
  pepper

Prepare all the vegetables, taking special care with the cucumber and horseradish as these will be the centerpiece of your finished salad. On a large, round serving plate, arrange the tuna fish in a round, and then form a rose shape on top of the fish by interlacing cucumber and horseradish slices. In a blender or food processor, purée the olives, scallions, mint leaves, olive oil, Tabasco, vinegar, salt and pepper until smooth. Place the shredded lettuce around the rose, followed by the tomatoes, and then pour the olive and mint mixture over the salad.

SURPRISE POTATOES

Choose large new potatoes for this dish, and take care not to break the skins when scooping out the centers.

Serves 8

INGREDIENTS

1 red bell pepper, seeded and
   cut into thin strips
1 tablespoon olive oil
4 pounds new potatoes, steamed
   (but not peeled)
½ cup butter
Scant 1 cup heavy cream
Salt and freshly ground black
   pepper

Preheat the oven to 400°F. Cook the bell pepper strips in the olive oil over a high heat for a few minutes. Remove from the heat, and set aside. Cut the potatoes in half, and remove the centers with a teaspoon. Leave enough potato with the skins for them to hold their shape. Mix the butter, cream, salt and pepper into the potato that you have scooped out, then stir in the bell pepper strips. Spoon the mixture back into the skins, and reheat in the oven for 5-8 minutes. Serve piping hot.

SALADE PAYSANNE

*This salad can be made from any selection of vegetables –
your favorites or those in season. Cut some of the vegetables
diagonally to make the salad as attractive as possible.*

Serves 6

INGREDIENTS
4 scallions
½ cucumber
3 carrots
6 large tomatoes
10 button mushrooms
3 stalks celery
1 green bell pepper, seeded and
  chopped
15–20 tiny cauliflower florets
15–20 radishes
1 tablespoon chopped watercress
2 sprigs cilantro leaf, or parsley
½ teaspoon salt
½ teaspoon freshly ground black
  pepper
2 tablespoons cider vinegar
1 tablespoon lemon juice
4 tablespoons olive or vegetable
  oil
Pinch of mustard powder
Sugar to taste
8 lettuce leaves for garnish

Trim the scallions and cut them
diagonally into thin slices. Peel
the cucumber, and quarter it
lengthwise. Use a sharp knife to
remove the soft, seedy center;
discard this, and dice the
remaining flesh. Peel the carrots,
and slice them thinly, cutting
them diagonally with a sharp
knife.

Cut a small cross into the skin of
each tomato, and plunge into
boiling water for 30 seconds.
Remove the tomatoes, and
carefully peel away the blanched
skin from the fruit. Quarter the
skinned tomatoes, and cut away
the tough green stalk. Thinly
slice the mushrooms and celery.
Cut the bell pepper in half
lengthwise and remove all the
seeds and white pith. Discard
this, and chop the flesh. Break
the cauliflower flowerets into
small pieces, quarter the
radishes, and roughly chop the
watercress, along with the
cilantro leaves or parsley.

Mix together all the remaining
ingredients, except the lettuce
leaves. Whisk thoroughly using a
fork, or balloon whisk, until the
mixture becomes a thick, cloudy
dressing.

Arrange the lettuce leaves on a
serving dish, and pile the
prepared vegetables on top.
Spoon a little of the dressing
over the salad just before serving,
and pass the remainder
separately in a small jug.

GLAZED VEGETABLES

This method of preparing vegetables is especially suited to root vegetables such as carrots, turnips, rutabagas and parsnips. However, the addition of cucumber makes a most refreshing contrast.

Serves 6

INGREDIENTS
1 pound carrots
1 large cucumber
1 pound turnips
¼ cup butter
9 sugar cubes
Salt and freshly ground black
    pepper

Wash and peel the vegetables as necessary. Cut them into long oval shapes with a sharp knife. Melt the butter in a large skillet, and add the vegetables, sugar, salt and pepper. Stir, adding just enough water to cover the vegetables. Cook over a high heat, letting the water evaporate. Let the vegetables caramelize a little, and then serve. Care should be taken as some vegetables cook more quickly than others. If time permits, cook the vegetables separately.

FRENCH BEANS PROVENÇAL HARICOTS VERTS À LA PROVENÇALE

This dish is traditionally made with haricots verts – French beans. It is also, however, a wonderful way of cooking string beans toward the end of their season.

Serves 7

INGREDIENTS
¼ cup butter
3 tablespoons olive oil
Bouquet garni
1 clove garlic, chopped
6 large tomatoes, seeded and
  chopped
2 onions, chopped
3 pounds French beans, topped
  and tailed
Salt and freshly ground black
  pepper

Garnish
½ clove garlic, finely chopped
1 tablespoon freshly chopped
  parsley

Heat the butter and oil together in a large skillet. Add the bouquet garni, garlic, tomatoes and onions, and cook for 20-30 minutes, or until very soft.

Cook the beans in boiling salted water until just cooked but still crisp. Rinse them immediately under cold running water to stop further cooking. Drain well, and add salt and pepper. Remove the bouquet garni from the tomatoes. Serve the beans on a bed of the tomato purée, and garnish with the chopped garlic and parsley.

CARROT PURÉE

Vegetable purées come and go in food fashions around the world, but they have always been popular in France. I sometimes add a little grated cheese to the purée.

Serves 6

INGREDIENTS
3 pounds carrots, sliced
1 tablespoon ground cinnamon
½ cup butter
⅔ cup heavy cream
Salt and freshly ground black pepper
Juice of half a lemon

Cook the carrots in boiling salted water until soft. Drain well, then press the carrots through a fine strainer or purée in a blender. Return the purée to the heat in a clean saucepan, and stir in the cinnamon, butter, cream, salt and pepper. Beat well with a wooden spoon, and heat thoroughly. Serve in a warmed dish with the lemon juice squeezed over.

RATATOUILLE

Ratatouille is one of the most famous French vegetable dishes, a stew of Mediterranean vegetables. There are many different recipes – in this one the vegetables are fried, which helps them to retain their individual flavors.

Serves 6

INGREDIENTS

3 eggplants, diced
4 zucchini, diced
1 red bell pepper, seeded and
    diced
1 green bell pepper, seeded and
    diced
12 baby onions
4 large tomatoes, seeded and
    diced
3 cloves garlic, chopped
5 cups olive oil
Sprig thyme
1 bay leaf
Salt and freshly ground black
    pepper

Prepare all the vegetables, taking care to retain all the juice from the tomatoes when removing the seeds. Set the oil to heat in a large skillet. Fry the eggplants in the oil until just brown. Remove and drain well. Leave on paper towels. Fry the zucchini and drain well; then fry the red and green bell peppers, and drain well. Finally, fry the baby onions, and drain well.

Put all the cooked vegetables into a heavy-bottomed saucepan with the garlic, tomatoes, any tomato juice recovered during seeding, the sprig of thyme, bay leaf, salt and pepper, 2 tablespoons water and 2 tablespoons of the frying oil. Cover the pan, and cook for 45- 60 minutes over a very low heat. Stir occasionally to prevent sticking. Remove the thyme and bay leaf before serving, and add salt and pepper to taste.

TOMATOES FROM LANGUEDOC

This dish is a celebration of ripe tomatoes and fresh juicy garlic. I could easily eat this on toast for lunch!

Serves 4

INGREDIENTS

4 large ripe tomatoes
Salt and freshly ground black
  pepper
2 tablespoons olive oil
1 clove garlic, crushed
2 slices white bread, crusts
  removed
1 tablespoon freshly chopped
  parsley
2 teaspoons freshly chopped
  thyme or marjoram

Cut the tomatoes in half, and score the cut surface. Sprinkle with salt, and leave upside-down in a colander to drain. Let the tomatoes drain for 1-2 hours. Rinse the tomatoes, and scoop out most of the juice and pulp. Mix the olive oil and garlic together, and brush both sides of the bread with the mixture, leaving it to soften. Chop the herbs and bread together until well mixed.

Press the filling into the tomatoes, and sprinkle with the remaining garlic and olive oil mixture. Cook the tomatoes in an ovenproof dish under a preheated broiler at a low heat for 5 minutes, then raise the dish or the heat to brown the tomatoes on top. Serve immediately.

FAVA BEANS WITH HAM

I am often surprised by how few French people know of fava beans – one of my favorite vegetables. Yet they grow happily and plentifully in France, as this recipe from Touraine, the fertile lands south of the Loire, shows.

Serves 6

INGREDIENTS
5 cups shelled fava beans
⅔ cup heavy cream
2 ounces ham, cut into strips
Salt and freshly ground black
   pepper
1 tablespoon freshly chopped
   parsley or chervil

If using fresh beans, remove them from their pods. Cook the beans in boiling salted water until tender; drain and keep them warm. Combine the cream and ham in a small saucepan. Add a pinch of salt and pepper, and bring to a boil. Boil rapidly for 5 minutes to thicken the cream. If wished, peel the outer skins from the beans before tossing them with the cream and ham. Add the parsley or chervil. Adjust the seasoning, and reheat if necessary. Serve immediately.

PETITS POIS BONNE FEMME

This recipe title quite literally means "housewive's peas." Oh!
that all housewives were so inventive!! Baby onions and
crispy bacon provide contrasts in both flavor and texture.

Serves 6

INGREDIENTS
3 cups chopped smoked bacon
¼ cup butter
2¼ pounds fresh peas (about 7
  pounds in the pod)
12 pearl onions
2 teaspoons sugar
Salt and freshly ground black
  pepper

Cook the chopped bacon in half the butter, then add the peas and just enough water to cover. Heat until just cooked, then drain well. Glaze the pearl onions. Cover them with water in a clean saucepan. Add the sugar and the remaining butter, and season with salt and pepper. Cook over a medium heat until the juice has reduced and is lightly coating the onions (like a syrup). Add the pearl onions to the peas just before serving.

SALADE NIÇOISE

*As with so many of the classic dishes of the world, the
definitive recipe for Salade Niçoise is muddled with the
many popular variations on a theme. I sometimes use green
beans and cold potatoes in place of the cucumber and
artichokes, but it is delicious any way!*

Serves 4–6

Ingredients
1 romaine lettuce
2 hard-cooked eggs, quartered
2 large tomatoes, quartered
6 anchovy fillets
10 black olives, pitted
1 tablespoon capers
¼ cucumber, diced but not
  peeled
7-ounce can tuna fish, drained
4 large artichoke hearts,
  quartered

Dressing
6 tablespoons olive oil
2 tablespoons white or red wine
  vinegar
½ clove garlic, crushed
1 teaspoon mustard
Salt, freshly ground black pepper
  and lemon juice

Wash the lettuce well, and pat
dry. Tear into small pieces.
Prepare the remaining salad
ingredients, and toss with the
lettuce in a large bowl, taking
care not to break up the eggs.
Mix the dressing ingredients
together, and whisk until well
emulsified. Pour the dressing
over the salad just before serving.

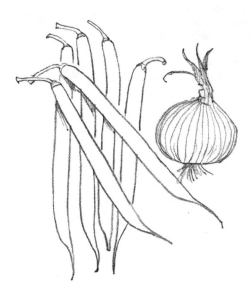

FRENCH BEANS WITH ONION

Such a simple recipe and such a delicious result! This method could be used for cooking any type of green bean: fava, snap or string.

Serves 4-6

INGREDIENTS
1 pound thin green beans
1 medium onion
2 tablespoons butter
Salt and freshly ground black
   pepper

Top and tail the beans, then cook them whole in boiling salted water for about 8–10 minutes. Meanwhile, finely chop the onion. Melt the butter, and fry the onion until lightly browned. Drain the beans, and toss them over the heat to dry. Pour the butter and onions over the beans, and season with salt and pepper. Serve immediately.

SALADE BRESSE

The rich blue cheese dressing makes this a sophisticated salad. It is at its best in the fall, when the new crop of walnuts reaches the market stalls.

Serves 4-6

INGREDIENTS

1 head radicchio leaves, separated and washed
1 romaine lettuce, washed
1 bunch of corn salad or watercress, washed
4 ounces cherry tomatoes, halved and cored
4 chicken breasts, cooked, skinned and thinly sliced
4 ounces Bresse Bleu, or other blue cheese, cut into small pieces
16 small pickled gherkins, thinly sliced
½ cup walnut halves
2 tablespoons vegetable oil
2 tablespoons walnut oil
2 teaspoons white wine vinegar
¾ cup fromage frais
2 teaspoons freshly chopped tarragon
Salt and freshly ground black pepper

Tear the radicchio and romaine lettuce into small pieces. Pull apart the corn salad, but leave the leaves whole. If using watercress, remove any thick stems and yellow leaves. Toss the lettuces together in a large salad bowl. Arrange the tomatoes, chicken, cheese, gherkins and walnuts on top of the lettuce, and mix gently.

Put the oils and vinegar together into a small bowl, and whisk well, until they are thick. Fold in the fromage frais and the tarragon. Whisk well, then season to taste. Drizzle some of the dressing over the salad before serving. Place the remaining dressing in a small jug and hand it round separately.

PETITS POIS À LA FRANÇAISE

It is most unusual to cook lettuce, but this is a classic way of cooking peas. The shredded lettuce really does add to the dish, and make it special.

Serves 6

INGREDIENTS

2¼ pounds fresh peas (about 7 pounds in the pod)
¼ cup butter
1 lettuce, finely shredded
6 onions, finely chopped
2 teaspoons sugar
Bouquet garni
Salt and freshly ground black pepper
2 carrots, finely diced

Rinse the peas under cold running water, and let them drain. Melt the butter in a heavy-bottomed saucepan, and cook the peas, lettuce, onions, sugar, bouquet garni, salt and pepper over a low heat for 5 minutes. Increase the heat, and add 1 inch of water. Bring to a boil and add the carrots. Cover the saucepan, and reduce the heat to very low; cook for 15-20 minutes; or until the peas are cooked through. Remove the bouquet garni, and serve.

DESSERTS

Desserts are an excuse. An excuse for what? Well, that's up to you, but for most of us desserts are an excuse for self-indulgence, for wallowing in gorgeous confections that might well be bad for us but really finish a meal perfectly, leaving us comforted and replete!

For simplicity, choose ripe fresh fruit in a state of utter perfection, and serve it, when appropriate, in a bowl of ice water. If you like to spend time in the kitchen on making intricate decorations, then some desserts will suit your inclinations. There are also ideal desserts for you to make if you prefer something simple and fruity that can be prepared ahead, such as an ice cream, a sorbet or a cold soufflé. And, if you are a chocoholic, what better excuse could there be for spending a little time in the kitchen than producing the most fantastic, wicked chocolate tart?

Simple Desserts in Delectable Combinations

The ingredients for desserts are seldom complicated in themselves. There are a few standard compilations which are used extensively, especially in classic French desserts, which are simple to make but add amazing depths. *Crème pâtissière* or pastry cream, caramel and praline are almost basic ingredients in so many recipes, but might appear offputting if you are not already an experienced cook. Do not let these things daunt you – they are all easy to prepare and will open the door to many of the great desserts of France if you can master them. Recipes for all of these can be found in the chapter on Basic Recipes at the end of this book.

Three Basic Skills

Crème pâtissière is a rich, set egg custard, and may be used in place of cream to fill pastry tarts before covering them with fresh fruits in season. It may be flavored with a little liqueur, and may also be lightened by the addition of just a little whipped cream. I love using this pastry cream, and find it much less rich than desserts which are stuffed full of dairy cream.

Caramel is used in so many ways – burned over custards, pulled into strands over choux buns, set and crushed in ice creams and for dipping ripe fruits for petits fours. It is so versatile. Praline is one stage on from caramel, and includes nuts. It is crushed or ground before being added to creamy fillings or being used for decoration.

Sugar, the Basic Ingredient of Desserts

Desserts didn't really become popular until the late fifteenth and sixteenth centuries. Until that time honey was the main sweetener in use throughout Europe, but sugar had, in fact, been in common use in India since the fifth century B.C. When first introduced to Europe, sugar was very expensive, and the inclusion of any sweet dishes at banquets and parties was more to show the extent of the host's wealth than anything else.

France, with its great tradition of experimentation in gastronomy, was able to lead in the development of many of the classic desserts now familiar throughout the world.

Some of my Favorite Desserts!

Yes, a lot of them are French, and most of them are included in this chapter! Crême brûlée, a rich custard with a burned sugar topping, chocolate roulade, strawberry tarts, profiteroles, Normandy apple tarts and tarte au citron – I love them all! Sheer and utter self-indulgence maybe, but each and every one of them provides the perfect ending to a meal. Of course, which meal may hold the key to the ultimate success of the dessert – don't choose something heavy and rich to serve after a rich main course. Selecting a dessert is just as important as planning the other courses of your meal.

A Secret Society?

Two sisters by the name of Tatin ran the Hôtel Terminus in Lamotte-Beuvron, in the Loire. They often produced an apple tart, and one day, by mistake, one of the sisters placed the apples that she had caramelized with butter and sugar into a pie pan which she had omitted to line with pastry dough. Rather than scoop it all out, she simply covered the apples with the pastry dough and inverted the tart onto a serving plate when cooked. Like so many great discoveries, Tarte Tatin was a mistake! It is now, however, one of the most popular and fashionable desserts in France – there is even a Tarte Tatin Society in the sisters' home town with an avidly enthusiastic membership.

GRAPEFRUIT AND WILD STRAWBERRY DUO

Lightly poached fresh grapefruit with a fresh wild strawberry sauce make a simple yet stylish dessert.

Serves 6

INGREDIENTS
5 grapefruit
1¼ cups Muscat wine
¼ cup sugar
3 cups wild strawberries, washed and hulled

Peel four of the grapefruits, removing all the white pith and cut into quarters. Squeeze the remaining grapefruit for its juice.

Put the Muscat wine and half the sugar in a saucepan, and let reduce by half. Add the grapefruit quarters, and poach for 1 minute, then remove them using a draining spoon. Stir in the juice of the remaining grapefruit. Crush the wild strawberries with the remaining sugar, and spread this paste over a serving plate. Lay the poached grapefruit quarters over the paste, and serve the sauce separately in a small serving jug.

BANANAS IN ORANGE SAUCE

The delicious caramel orange sauce makes this a perfect dish hot or cold. To obtain a really authentic flavor, use French Rivesaltes in place of the sherry.

Serves 6

INGREDIENTS
2 tablespoons butter
3 tablespoons sugar
1 tablespoon cream sherry
2 tablespoons orange liqueur
Juice of 2 oranges
6 large bananas, peeled

In a heavy-bottomed saucepan, melt the butter and sugar together over a gentle heat. When dissolved, increase the heat, and boil the mixture until a white caramel forms. Carefully stir in the sherry, liqueur and orange juice, and let the mixture reduce a little. Cut the bananas into equal slices, and add them to the sauce.

With a tablespoon, remove the sauce-coated bananas, and arrange them on individual plates. Make rose shapes by interlacing the bananas, then pour over the remaining sauce.

GÂTEAUX GIENNOIS

Nutty-flavored, fluffy-topped tarts, with a surprise raspberry center.

Serves 4

INGREDIENTS

8 ounces sweet pastry dough
  (see recipe)
3 egg yolks
½ cup superfine sugar
Generous ½ cup ground shelled
  walnuts
2 egg whites, stiffly beaten
4 tablespoons raspberry jam

Preheat the oven to 350°F. Roll out the dough on a lightly floured counter, and use it to line 4 individual pie pans, pricking the bottoms and sides with a fork. Beat together the egg yolks and the sugar until pale, then stir in the ground walnuts. Gently incorporate the beaten egg whites, using a metal spoon. Place 1 tablespoon of the jam in the bottom of each tart, and spoon over the mixture dividing it evenly between the 4 tarts. Bake until the pastry is cooked and the filling lightly puffed, about 20 minutes. Serve as soon as possible.

CRÈME BRÛLÉE

I always tease a friend of mine who invariably serves Crème Brûlée whenever we eat with her – but we don't really mind because it is delicious! Fresh fruit may be hidden under the custard.

Serves 6-8

INGREDIENTS
4 egg yolks
1 teaspoon cornstarch
¼ cup superfine sugar
Vanilla extract
1¼ cups heavy cream
1¼ cups light cream

Caramel
⅓ cup granulated sugar
3 tablespoons water

Blend the egg yolks, cornstarch, superfine sugar and a little vanilla extract together in a bowl. Heat the creams until they reach boiling point, then pour onto the egg yolks, stirring all the time with a wooden spoon. Mix well, and return the mixture to the saucepan over a low heat. Stir continuously until the cream has thickened. This will take a few minutes. If the cream overheats, remove the pan from the heat, and beat until it becomes smooth. Divide the mixture between six ramekins, or pour it into a soufflé dish. Let cool, then cover with plastic wrap, and refrigerate overnight.

Put the sugar and water into a pan over a low heat until the sugar dissolves. Boil until golden-brown in color. Pour the caramel carefully over the creams, and chill until required.

Alternatively, sprinkle the top of the chilled cream with granulated sugar, covering the surface completely with the sugar. Place under a very hot broiler until the sugar melts and turns golden, but do not let it burn. Return the crème brûlée to the refrigerator until needed.

CŒUR À LA CRÈME

*These creamy desserts are traditionally made in
heart-shaped molds, making a very romantic dessert!
However, individual ramekins work just as well.*

Serves 6

INGREDIENTS
1 pound creamed cottage cheese
½ cup superfine sugar
Grated rind of 1 lemon
3 large ripe peaches
Juice of ½ lemon
2 tablespoons orange liqueur
4 tablespoons dry white wine
6 ripe strawberries for decoration

Combine the creamed cottage
cheese, sugar and lemon rind
together in a bowl (this can also
be done in a food processor).
Press the mixture into six molds,
and chill for 4-6 hours.

Meanwhile, skin, halve and pit
the peaches. Liquidize the flesh
in a blender, and mix in the
lemon juice, orange liqueur and
dry white wine.

When you are ready to serve,
invert the molds onto flat plates,
and spoon a little peach purée
around each one. Partly slice
each strawberry and fan them
out to decorate each plate.

Many different fruits could be
used with the cœur à la crème –
plums and raspberries both work
well, and blueberries, although
not so traditional, make a
dramatic contrast in color.

CHOCOLATE ROULADE

*A roulade is merely a culinary term for a roll with a filling.
Roulades may be sweet or savory, but chocolate is my
favorite!*

Serves 8–10

INGREDIENTS
5 eggs, separated
1 cup superfine sugar
6 squares dark chocolate
2 tablespoons water
Confectioners' sugar

Filling
1¼ cups heavy cream flavored
  with a liqueur or vanilla
  extract, lightly whipped

Preheat the oven to 350°F. Line a shallow jelly roll pan with baking parchment.

Separate the eggs, and beat the yolks into the sugar until the mixture is pale yellow. Melt the chocolate with the water in a bowl over a pan of water over a low heat, or melt in a microwave on defrost for 6 minutes. Beat the melted chocolate into the egg yolk and sugar mixture. Beat the egg whites until very firm, and fold them into the chocolate mixture. Pour the mixture into the prepared pan and carefully level the surface. Bake the roulade for 20 minutes.

Remove the roulade from the oven, and let cool slightly. Cover with a clean dish cloth wrung out in cold water; this is to prevent a hard crust from forming. Place the roulade in the refrigerator, and chill for 12-24 hours.

Lay a piece of baking parchment on a flat surface, and dust with confectioners' sugar. Tip out the roulade upside down onto the prepared paper, and remove the oiled baking parchment. Cover the roulade with the whipped cream, and roll it up like a jelly roll. Dust with a little extra confectioners' sugar. Keep chilled until ready to serve.

This roulade freezes very well, and thaws in just a few hours.

FRESH FRUIT CREAM

This is an unusual but simple dessert, memorable yet quick to prepare. The creamy custard topping is browned quickly under a hot broiler – a variation on crème brûlée.

Serves 6

INGREDIENTS
1¼ cups crème pâtissière (see recipe)
2 tablespoons Kirsch
1 cup whipping cream, whipped with 2 tablespoons superfine sugar
Seasonal fresh fruit, peeled, pitted, sliced or cubed (enough for 6 servings)

Preheat the oven to 375°F. Gently mix together the crème pâtissière, Kirsch and 2 tablespoons of the whipped cream, then, using a metal spoon, carefully fold in the remaining cream.

Arrange the fruit in an ovenproof dish, and spoon over the topping. Cook for 10 minutes in the oven. Transfer to a hot broiler, and let the top crisp until brown. Serve immediately.

OPEN FRUIT TART

JALOUSIE DES FRUITS

This was one of the first classic French desserts that I was taught at cookery college to practice using puff or flaky pastry. It is simple, spectacular and delicious.

Serves 4-6

INGREDIENTS
14 ounces puff pastry
Egg for glazing
Assorted fruit, such as 3-4
    peaches, 1 cup cherries, 1 cup
    strawberries, 1 cup grapes
3 tablespoons jam (apricot is
    good as it does not mask the
    color of the fruits, but if all red
    fruits are used, use raspberry
    jam)
1 tablespoon lemon juice

Preheat the oven to 425°F. Roll out the dough into a large rectangle about ¼ inch thick. Using a sharp knife, cut strips of dough 1 inch wide from all sides of the rectangle. Transfer the rectangle to a dampened baking sheet, and, moisten the edges with cold water. Lay the strips along the edges (make sure they are neatly trimmed), and press down lightly to seal the surfaces. Prick the bottom with a fork, leaving the edging strips plain. Flute or crimp the edges with a knife or finger and thumb, and glaze with a little beaten egg. Bake the dough in the oven for 15-20 minutes, until risen and golden. Remove from the oven, and let cool on a wire rack.

Slice the peaches. Pit the cherries, seed the grapes and leave the strawberries whole. Place the fruit carefully in rows according to size or color. Meanwhile, place the jam in a small saucepan together with the lemon juice, and bring to a boil, stirring continuously. Let cool but not reset. (If it is too thick, add a little boiling water.) Using a brush, liberally coat the fruit with the jam glaze.

Do not assemble this dessert too far in advance – leave it as late as possible, not more than 1-2 hours before serving.

As an alternative, fill the bottom with 1¼ cups of crème pâtissière (see recipe) or whipped heavy cream, and top with the fruits.

CRÊPES SUZETTE

This is the classic dish of paper-thin pancakes flamed and flavored with orange liqueur. With a well used and trusted skillet, this is a very easy and impressive recipe to prepare.

Serves 4 (Allow about 3 crêpes per person)

INGREDIENTS
Crêpe Batter
2 cups milk and water mixed
4 eggs
Pinch of salt
2 cups all-purpose flour, sifted
1 tablespoon sugar
4 tablespoons melted butter or oil

Orange Butter
¼ cup butter
¼ cup superfine sugar
Grated peel of 1 orange
1-2 tablespoons Grand Marnier or Curaçao

To Flame
2 tablespoons brandy
2 tablespoons Grand Marnier or Curaçao
2-3 tablespoons butter

Put all the ingredients for the crêpes into a blender or food processor, and blend for about 1 minute, pushing down the ingredients from the sides occasionally. Process a few seconds more to blend thoroughly. Leave, covered, in a cool place for 30-60 minutes. The consistency of the batter should be that of light cream. Add more milk if necessary. Brush a crêpe pan or small skillet, lightly with oil, and place over a high heat. When a slight haze forms, pour a large spoonful of the batter into the pan, and swirl the pan to cover the bottom. Pour out any excess into a separate bowl. Cook on one side until just beginning to brown around the edges. Turn over, and cook on the other side until lightly speckled with brown. Slide each crêpe onto a plate, and repeat using the remaining batter. Reheat the pan occasionally in between cooking the crêpes. The amount of batter should make 12 crêpes.

For the orange butter, beat together the butter, sugar and grated orange peel until light and fluffy. Add the orange liqueur, and spread a little of this orange butter on one side of each crêpe.

To flame the crêpes, put the brandy and orange liqueur into a small saucepan ready to flame them at the last moment.

Melt the butter in a large skillet. Add a crêpe, orange butter-side down, and cook very quickly for 30 seconds. Fold in half and half again into the traditional triangular shape, and put to one side of the pan. Repeat until all the crêpes are cooked.

Heat the liqueur in the small saucepan; set alight, and pour over the crêpes. Serve at once.

PEACH MELBA

One of the classic desserts, created by Escoffier in 1893 to honour the soprano, Dame Nellie Melba. Served with a raspberry coulis, this dessert is one of summer's pleasures.

Serves 6

INGREDIENTS
¾ cup granulated sugar
Juice of half a lemon
1 tablespoon Kirsch
1 pound fresh raspberries
6 fresh, ripe peaches, skinned, or whole canned peaches in syrup
2½ cups vanilla ice cream

Put 1¼ cups of water into a saucepan with the sugar, lemon juice, Kirsch and raspberries. Boil briskly for 5 minutes, then set aside to cool. When cool, purée in a blender or food processor then press through a fine strainer. Chill.

Place each peach in a small bowl, and add a scoop of ice cream. Spoon over a little of the raspberry sauce.

APPLES WITH MUSCAT DE BEAUMES DE VENISE

Muscat de Beaumes de Venise is one of the best known of all dessert wines. It is the most marvelous ingredient to cook with for special occasions.

Serves 4

INGREDIENTS
¼ cup butter
4 eating apples, peeled and quartered
¼ cup superfine sugar
3 tablespoons currants
½ cup Muscat de Beaumes de Venise
1 teaspoon cinnamon

Melt the butter in a large skillet, and cook the apples until lightly browned; then add the sugar, and let caramelize slightly. Sprinkle with the currants, and cook for a few seconds more. Add the wine, and boil until slightly reduced; then sprinkle with the cinnamon, and serve immediately.

FRESH FRUIT IN RED WINE SYRUP

*Pears are traditionally prepared by poaching in red wine.
This method creates a contemporary variation of the classic
recipe, and uses fruits that do not require poaching
or cooking.*

Serves 8

INGREDIENTS
2¼ cups light red wine
   (Beaujolais or similar)
Scant 1 cup water
2 cups granulated sugar
1 clove
Zest of 1 orange
1 stick cinnamon
A selection of fresh fruit, peeled,
   pitted, sliced or halved as
   necessary

Make a syrup by boiling together
the wine, water, sugar, clove,
orange zest and cinnamon for at
least 30 minutes. Remove from
the heat, and set aside to cool,
chill.

Prepare the fruit, and arrange it
on a serving dish or in a bowl.
Remove the cinnamon and clove
from the syrup, and pour the
chilled liquid over the fruit.
Serve.

SOUFFLÉ AU CITRON FROID

This is one of my favorite desserts – it is very easy to make (although it requires several bowls) and has a refreshing tang. Use heavy or whipping cream – I find the latter gives a lighter result. You should be able to write a four-letter word across the egg yolk mixture when it is sufficiently well beaten and thickened.

Serves 6

INGREDIENTS
3 eggs, separated
175g/6oz sugar
Grated rind and juice of 2 small lemons
1 tablespoon gelatin soaked in 3-4 tablespoons hot water
¾ cup cream, lightly whipped

Decoration
⅔ cup cream, whipped
Finely chopped almonds or pistachios
Thin strips lemon rind or lemon twists

Tie a double thickness of baking parchment around a soufflé dish to stand about 3 inches above the rim of the dish, and set aside.

Beat the egg yolks in a large bowl. Add the sugar gradually and the lemon rind and juice. Set the bowl over a pan of hot water, and whisk until the mixture is thick, and leaves a ribbon trail. Remove the bowl from the heat, and whisk for a few minutes longer. Dissolve the gelatin in the water until clear; pour it into the lemon mixture, and stir thoroughly. Set the bowl over ice and stir until beginning to thicken.

Beat the egg whites until stiff but not dry, and fold into the lemon mixture along with the lightly whipped cream. Pour into the prepared soufflé dish, and chill until the soufflé is set. To decorate, peel off the paper carefully, and thinly spread some of the cream on the sides of the soufflé. Press finely chopped nuts into the cream. Pipe the remaining cream into rosettes on top of the soufflé, and decorate with strips of rind or lemon twists.

195

BASQUE CHOCOLATE MOUSSE
MOUSSE AU CHOCOLAT BASQUE

A rich, thick chocolate mousse – very simple to make and an all-time favorite dessert with everyone. Use a good-quality chocolate with at least 50 percent cocoa solids.

Serves 7

INGREDIENTS
6 squares dark chocolate
Scant ⅓ cup water
1 tablespoon butter
2 tablespoons rum
3 eggs, separated
Whipped cream and chocolate
  curls to decorate, optional

Chop or break the chocolate into small pieces, and combine with the water in a bowl over a heavy-based saucepan of water. Cook over a very gentle heat so that the chocolate and water form a thick cream. Remove the bowl from the heat. Let cool slightly, and then beat in the butter. Add the rum, and beat in the egg yolks one at a time.

Whisk the egg whites until stiff but not dry, and fold them gently into the chocolate mixture. Pour into small pots or ramekins, and chill for at least 2–3 hours. Finish with whipped cream and chocolate curls, if wished.

PANCAKES WITH CHOCOLATE RASPBERRIES

The French do not only use crêpes to make Crêpes Suzettes!! These rich, thin pancakes may be filled with almost any fruit and sauce of your choice – I like to use fresh raspberries in season, in place of the jam.

Serves 6

INGREDIENTS

Crêpe Batter
2 cups milk and water mixed
4 eggs
Pinch of salt
2 cups all-purpose flour, sifted
1 tablespoon sugar
4 tablespoons melted butter or
   oil

Filling
8 squares dark chocolate, grated
⅓ cup seedless raspberry jam

Decoration
Whipped cream and chopped,
   toasted hazelnuts

Preheat the oven to 350°F. Put all the ingredients for the crêpes into a blender or food processor, and blend for about 1 minute, pushing down the ingredients from the sides occasionally. Process for a few seconds more to blend thoroughly. Leave, covered, in a cool place for 30-60 minutes. The consistency of the batter should be that of light cream. Add more milk if necessary. Brush a crêpe pan or small skillet lightly with oil and place over a high heat. When a slight haze forms, pour a large spoonful of the batter into the pan, and swirl the pan to cover the base. Pour out any excess into a separate bowl. Cook on one side until just beginning to brown around the edges. Turn over and cook on the other side until lightly speckled with brown. Slide each crêpe onto a plate, and repeat using the remaining batter. Reheat the pan occasionally in between cooking the crêpes. The amount of batter should make 12 crêpes.

As the crêpes are cooked, sprinkle them evenly with grated chocolate, and divide the raspberry jam among them. Roll them up so that the jam shows at the ends, or fold into triangles. Reheat in the oven for about 10 minutes before serving. Top with whipped cream and a sprinkling of toasted nuts.

FRENCH APPLE FLAN

The most striking thing about French apple flans is the attractive arrangement of the sliced apple, and the fact that eating apples are most commonly used, not cooking apples. I leave the skin on the apples if it is red.

Serves 6

INGREDIENTS
¾ cup all-purpose flour
¾ cup self-rising flour
¼ cup butter
¼ cup margarine
¼ cup sifted confectioners' sugar
Cold water (about 2-3
   tablespoons)

Filling
4 tablespoons apricot jam
2 tablespoons water
Juice of 1 small lemon
1¼ pounds eating apples
1 tablespoon superfine sugar

Preheat the oven to 400°F. Put the flours into a bowl, then rub in the fats until the mixture resembles fine bread crumbs. Stir in the confectioners' sugar. Mix to form a firm but pliable dough with cold water. Knead the dough lightly on a floured surface until smooth. Roll out the dough, and use it to line a 9-9½-inch loose-bottomed French fluted flan pan.

To prepare the filling, boil together the jam and water for 2-3 minutes, stirring constantly. Strain the glaze into a cup to cool. Squeeze the lemon juice into a bowl. Peel, core and thinly slice the apples straight into the lemon juice. Arrange the apple slices neatly in the pie shell, overlapping them in rounds, and sprinkle with the sugar. Place the flan on a baking sheet, and bake for about 35 minutes. While still hot, brush the flan with the apricot glaze. Serve warm with heavy cream.

FLOATING ISLANDS

This might sound a bit daunting, but the poaching of
meringue islands is very straightforward. Just take care not
to overcook them, as they will dissolve away to nothing!

Serves 4

INGREDIENTS
6 egg whites
Pinch of salt
½ cup superfine sugar
2 cups milk
2 cups water
2 cups Egg Custard Sauce (see
  recipe)
2 tablespoons crushed Praline
  (see recipe)

Beat the egg whites with a pinch
of salt until light and foamy. Add
half the sugar, and beat until
almost stiff. Add the remaining
sugar, and continue beating until
stiff peaks form. Heat the milk
and water together over a
moderate heat. Place the
meringue mixture in a piping bag
without a tip and squeeze large
"islands" of meringue out onto a
spatula. If you do not have a
piping bag, simply use a
tablespoon to scoop out the
islands, and drop them directly
into the hot milk and water.
Lower each meringue island onto
the hot milk and water on the
spatula, and poach gently for
about 2 minutes, turning once –
the cooking time will depend on
the size of the islands. Do not
poach for too long, or they will
dissolve.

Remove the islands from the milk
and water, using a draining
spoon, and let them drain and
cool on a wire rack. To serve,
divide the custard sauce between
four dessert plates, place the
meringue islands on top, and
sprinkle with the crushed praline
before serving.

BRIOCHE FRENCH TOASTS

This is not a true classic dish, but I am certain that you will recognize the method! This makes a quick and economical family dessert.

Serves 4

INGREDIENTS
4 small brioches
4 tablespoons heavy cream
3 eggs
1 tablespoon sugar
1 teaspoon orange flower water
2 tablespoons melted butter
Confectioners' sugar
Egg Custard Sauce (see recipe)

Cut each small brioche into three slices. Beat together the cream, eggs, sugar and orange flower water. Dip each brioche slice quickly into the cream and egg mixture, making sure both sides are coated.

Melt a little of the butter at a time, and sauté the dipped slices in batches, cooking the toasts for about 2 minutes on each side, until golden-brown. Serve each batch immediately, sprinkled with a little sifted confectioners' sugar and surrounded by egg custard sauce.

STRAWBERRIES ESCOFFIER
FRAISES ESCOFFIER

The combination of strawberries and sweet oranges is delicious and well worthy of the great chef Escoffier.

Serves 4

INGREDIENTS
2 pounds strawberries
2 oranges
¼ cup sugar cubes
Scant ⅓ cup Grand Marnier

Hull and slice the strawberries. Peel, removing all the white pith, and slice the oranges. Mash half the strawberries with the sugar and Grand Marnier, then stir in the remaining strawberries and the oranges. Chill the fruit mixture for 1 hour, then serve in individual glasses.

CHOCOLATE SOUFFLÉ

Hot soufflés create a big impression on friends and family, and are actually very easy to prepare. Chocolate soufflé is lighter than chocolate mousse. Both are definitely classic French desserts.

Serves 4

INGREDIENTS
Melted butter
Sugar
2 eggs, 1 separated
½ cup superfine sugar
2 tablespoons all-purpose flour
1 heaped tablespoon cocoa
  powder
1 cup milk
4 egg whites
Pinch of salt
Confectioners' sugar

Preheat the oven to 400°F. Grease four ramekins with the melted butter, and sprinkle with sugar, shaking out any excess.

Beat 1 whole egg plus 1 egg white with the sugar, and then beat in the flour and the cocoa powder. Bring the milk to a boil in a small saucepan, then pour it over the egg mixture, stirring continuously. Return the mixture to the saucepan, and stir it continuously over a low heat until it has thickened and is just coming to a boil. Remove from the heat, and let cool. When cool, add the remaining egg yolk, and mix well.

Beat the egg whites with a pinch of salt until stiff. Mix a little of the egg white into the soufflé mixture to lighten it, and then fold in the remaining egg white gently but thoroughly. Fill the ramekins with the soufflé mixture, and bake for about 20 minutes, until well risen and firm. Remove from the oven, and sprinkle quickly with confectioners' sugar. Serve immediately, before the soufflés fall.

BLACKCURRANT SORBET

Sorbets and water ices are popular everywhere. This sorbet makes a light dessert, but sorbets are more commonly used in France to clear the palate between savory courses.

Serves 4-6

INGREDIENTS
2 pounds fresh or thawed frozen
  blackcurrants
1 cup sugar
1¼ cups water
2 egg whites

Put all the ingredients, except the egg whites, into a saucepan, and cook slowly over a low heat for 15 minutes. Press the fruit mixture through a strainer, then pour into a freezer-proof container with a lid. Freeze until mushy. Beat the egg whites until firm, and fold into the partly frozen blackcurrant mixture. Return to the freezer until almost frozen. If the sorbet becomes completely frozen and hard, put it into the refrigerator for 15 minutes to soften before serving.

PEAR CHARLOTTE

I always like to use fresh fruit in season (pears and peaches both work well in this dessert), but canned fruit may also be used. This is another of the classic desserts that looks daunting, but is really simple to make.

Serves 6

INGREDIENTS

4 large ripe pears, peeled and
  cored
2 tablespoons superfine sugar
⅔ cup apple juice
⅔ cup fromage frais
2 tablespoons gelatin
4 tablespoons pear liqueur
4 tablespoons water
1 cup heavy cream
14 lady-fingers
Melted chocolate, to decorate

Cut one pear into dice, and set aside. In a blender or food processor, purée the remaining pears with the sugar and apple juice. Add the fromage frais, and mix well.

Soften the gelatin in a little cold water, then put into a saucepan with 2 tablespoons of the pear liqueur and 2 tablespoons of the water. Stir over a low heat to dissolve. Do not let the gelatin mixture boil. Mix the dissolved gelatin into the fromage frais and pear purée. Whip the cream until thick, then fold into the pear mixture. Carefully fold in the reserved diced pear.

Mix together the remaining 2 tablespoons pear liqueur and 2 tablespoons water, and brush over the lady-fingers, then use them to line the bottom and sides of a charlotte mold or straight-sided cake pan. Turn the pear mousse into the lined mold. Let set in the refrigerator for at least 3 hours. Invert and serve chilled, decorated with a little melted chocolate.

STRAWBERRY MOUSSE

Light and refreshing, this is a classic dessert that enjoys enduring popularity.

Serves 4

INGREDIENTS

1 cup water
¾ cup superfine sugar
2 pounds fresh or frozen
   strawberries
2 tablespoons gelatin
⅔ cup heavy cream
Mint leaves, to decorate

Boil the water and sugar together for about 7 minutes to make a light syrup. Add half the strawberries, and set aside for about 15 minutes. Purée the mixture in a blender or food processor, then pass the purée through a strainer to remove the seeds.

Dice six of the remaining strawberries. Soften the gelatin in a little cold water. Measure ⅔ cup of the purée, and reheat if not hot; then add the gelatin and stir until it has completely dissolved. Add the diced strawberry, then set aside until the mixture is cool but not set. Whip the cream until thick. Fold it gently but thoroughly into the cooled strawberry mixture. Pour the mousse into four individual molds or one large mold, and let set in the refrigerator for at least 2 hours.

Prepare a purée from the remaining strawberries. Put them into a saucepan with ⅔ cup of water, and cook until soft. Press the pulp through a strainer, and sweeten to taste with sugar if necessary. Cool and chill. To serve, unmold the mousses onto individual serving plates, and surround with the strawberry purée. Decorate the mousses with small mint leaves.

PRUNE & ARMAGNAC MOUSSE

Prunes and Armagnac are both traditional foods in southwest France. The main prune area is around Agen, where the best prunes in the world are produced – well, that's my opinion! Delicious!

Serves 4

INGREDIENTS

1 cup fromage frais
1¼ cups Egg Custard Sauce (see recipe)
⅔ cup pitted prunes
1 tablespoon gelatin
2 tablespoons Armagnac, or to taste
⅔ cup heavy cream

Put the fromage frais and the custard sauce into a blender or food processor. Add the prunes, and process quickly. Transfer the mixture into a bowl. Soften the gelatin in a little cold water, then put into a small saucepan with an additional 2 tablespoons water and the Armagnac. Heat slowly, and stir until the gelatin dissolves. Pour the gelatin into the fromage frais mixture, and beat together well. Whip the cream until light and fluffy, then fold it gently into the prune custard.

Divide the mousse between four individual molds or ramekins, and let set in the refrigerator for at least 2 hours. Unmold and serve chilled.

206

PEAR OMELET

Sweet omelets are quite delicious. They are a classic French dessert, and deserve to be more popular outside France. Make certain that you use unsalted butter for cooking the omelet!

Serves 4

INGREDIENTS
4-5 ripe pears
12 eggs
2 tablespoons heavy cream
2 tablespoons superfine sugar
Pinch of ground cloves
Oil or unsalted butter

Peel, core and dice the pears. Beat the eggs with the cream and sugar. Add a pinch of ground cloves, and stir in the pears.

Heat about 2 tablespoons of oil or butter in a large omelet pan. When hot, pour in the egg mixture. Stir the mixture a little in the pan, then cook for a few minutes until set. Shake the omelet loose, and flip it over, as for a pancake, and cook on the other side. Serve warm, cut into quarters.

CHILLED GRAND MARNIER SOUFFLÉS

Grand Marnier is one of the best known of French liqueurs. It has an orange flavor and is excellent for cooking – as well as for drinking!

Serves 4

INGREDIENTS
6 egg yolks
½ cup superfine sugar
3 tablespoons Grand Marnier
6 egg whites
⅔ cup whipping cream

Prepare four ramekins: fix a "collar" of waxed paper around each one, securing the paper with tape or string. Put the egg yolks, sugar, Grand Marnier and 1 tablespoon of water into a bowl set over a saucepan of simmering water, and beat until the mixture forms a ribbon, a thick thread, if dropped from a spoon. Remove from the heat, and continue to beat until the mixture has cooled. Beat the egg whites until stiff peaks form. Whip the cream until light and fluffy.

Fold the egg whites gently into the egg mixture, so as not to lose any of the volume, and then fold in the whipped cream. Divide the mixture between the prepared ramekins. Let chill for at least 3 hours, or until set. Remove the paper collars from the ramekins just before serving.

FROZEN NOUGAT

Nougat is very typically French, either as a dessert or as a candy. It is very sweet, so only serve small portions.

Serves 6

INGREDIENTS
½ cup raisins
¾ cup candied fruit
2 tablespoons coconut liqueur
⅓ cup honey
4 teaspoons superfine sugar
2 tablespoons water
4 egg whites
⅔ cup heavy cream
2 tablespoons crushed Praline

Soak the raisins and the candied fruit in the coconut liqueur for at least 30 minutes. Boil the honey, sugar and water in a small saucepan for 3-4 minutes to obtain a thick syrup. Beat the egg whites until very stiff.

Gradually add the hot syrup to the egg whites, beating continuously until a thick, smooth meringue is obtained. Whip the cream, and fold it gently into the meringue mixture. Add the crushed praline, the raisins and candied fruit together with their marinade; stir gently.

Line a loaf pan with waxed paper. Pour in the nougat mixture, and freeze for 24 hours. To serve, remove the frozen nougat from the loaf pan, and discard the waxed paper. Cut the nougat into wedges or slices. Serve immediately.

CHOUX PUFFS WITH CARAMEL ICE CREAM

I don't know why no one seems to make a commercial caramel ice cream – it is so delicious! This is a modern variation of an old classic – a new way of serving profiteroles.

INGREDIENTS

Ice Cream
½ cup sugar
2 tablespoons water
½ cup water
1 cup Egg Custard Sauce (see recipe)

Choux Paste
2 tablespoons melted butter
½ cup water
1 teaspoon sugar
Pinch of salt
½ cup plus 2 tablespoons all-purpose flour
2 eggs, beaten

Make a caramel using the ½ cup sugar and the 2 tablespoons water (for method see recipe in Basic Recipes). When the sugar has caramelized, add the extra water, and return to the heat for 1 minute. Stir to mix, then set aside to cool. Combine the cooled caramel with the custard sauce, stirring together thoroughly; then pour into an ice cream maker, and process until the ice cream sets. Alternatively, pour the mixture into a freezing tray, and freeze for 2 hours. Remove from the freezer, and thoroughly beat the part-frozen mixture and then replace in the freezer until set.

Preheat the oven to 400°F. Lightly grease a baking sheet. To make the choux paste, bring the butter, the remaining water, the sugar and salt to a boil in a medium saucepan. When the mixture is boiling, tip in all the flour at once. Beat thoroughly, and cook the paste, stirring continuously, for another 2 minutes. Remove the paste from the heat; add the first egg, and beat until well mixed. Add the second egg, beating well to obtain a smooth, elastic dough – do not add all the egg if it is not required. Place the paste in a piping bag with a plain metal tip. Pipe balls of choux paste onto a greased baking sheet. Dip a fork in beaten egg, and slightly flatten each of the balls. Bake for about 20 minutes, or until lightly browned and well puffed. Remove from the oven, and set aside to cool.

Cut open the base of each choux puff, and spoon or pipe in a little of the caramel ice cream. Put the filled puffs into the freezer for 30 minutes before serving.

PEARS "BELLE HÉLÈNE"

This is probably the best-known of all the classic French desserts featuring pears – it is utterly delicious, a perfect combination of ingredients. The first recipe for Pears "Belle Hélène" may not have included ice cream – but I like it!

Serves 4

INGREDIENTS
4 large ripe pears
4 squares good dark chocolate
½ cup milk
2 teaspoons sugar
4 scoops vanilla ice cream
1 tablespoon toasted, slivered
   almonds

Cut the pears in half lengthwise, and remove all the seeds from the center with a melon baller or teaspoon. Cut each half pear into neat slices lengthwise.

Melt the chocolate with the milk and sugar in a bowl set over a saucepan of hot water. Mix together well. Fan out each pear on a serving plate. Pour the chocolate sauce around the edges, and top with a scoop of ice cream. Sprinkle with the almonds. Serve immediately.

STRAWBERRY TARTS

The French are famed for their pastries and especially for their fruit tarts. These have an almond-flavored cream instead of a traditional crème pâtissière filling.

Serves 4

Ingredients

Sweet Pastry Dough
1¼ cups all-purpose flour
¼ cup superfine sugar
½ egg yolk
2 tablespoons water
Pinch of salt
¼ cup softened butter

Almond Cream
½ cup softened butter
½ cup superfine sugar
½ cup ground almonds
1 egg

Topping
8-12 ounces strawberries, hulled and washed
3 tablespoons strawberry glaze, or melted strawberry jam

To make the pastry dough, mix together the flour, sugar, egg yolk, water and salt. Add the softened butter; mix thoroughly together, and form into a ball. Let rest in the refrigerator. Make the almond cream by beating together the butter and sugar until light. Add the ground almonds and egg; mix well, and set aside in the refrigerator. Dry the strawberries; trim as necessary, and slice neatly.

Preheat the oven to 400°F. Roll out the dough and use to line four individual nonstick pans, or one large one (about 8 inches in diameter) if preferred. Prick the bases with a fork. Either use a piping bag to pipe the almond cream into the tart shells or simply spoon in the cream, and spread it evenly with the back of the spoon. Bake for 20 minutes. When the tarts are cooked, let them cool and then arrange the strawberries decoratively over the cream. Brush the strawberries with the glaze, let them set for 30 minutes in the refrigerator. Serve chilled.

FRUIT SORBETS

There are two varieties of fruit sorbet, one with egg white and one without. Lighter and more refreshing than ice cream, these are excellent desserts to have in your freezer, ready for unexpected guests.

Serves 4-6

INGREDIENTS
Orange sorbet
1 cup plus 2 tablespoons
    superfine sugar
Zest of 1 orange
1¼ cups fresh orange juice
½ cup fresh lemon juice

Dissolve the sugar in 2½ cups water. Bring to a boil, and boil continuously for 10 minutes. Set aside to cool. Blanch the orange zest in boiling water, for 15 seconds. Mix the cooled syrup with the orange and lemon juice, and stir in the zest. Pour the mixture into a plastic container, and place in the freezer. Remove the sorbet from the freezer every 30 minutes, and beat with a fork until it has completely crystallized.

INGREDIENTS
Pear Sorbet
¼ cup plus 1 tablespoon
    superfine sugar
1 pound pears, peeled and
    chopped
3 tablespoons lemon juice
1 egg white and a pinch of salt

Dissolve the sugar in ⅔ cup water. Add the chopped pear; then bring to a boil, and boil continuously for 10 minutes. Set aside to cool. When cool, purée in a blender or food processor until smooth. Stir in the lemon juice, and pour into a plastic container. Freeze for 1 hour.

After 1 hour, remove the sorbet, and beat it well with a fork. Beat the egg white with the salt until stiff. Fold gently into the sorbet, using a metal spoon. Cover and return to the freezer until needed.

POACHED PEARS IN PORT

This is the classic way of poaching pears in red wine or port. Choose even-size pears with stalks – this makes them more attractive for serving.

Serves 4

INGREDIENTS
Juice of 1 lemon
4 large firm pears, peeled
2½ cups port or red wine and
   port, mixed
1 teaspoon ground cinnamon
Generous 1 cup superfine sugar

Pour the lemon juice over the peeled pears – this will prevent them from discoloring. Place the pears in a large saucepan, add the port and just enough water to cover. Sprinkle over the cinnamon and the sugar, and cook over a gentle heat for 15-20 minutes until just cooked. Remove the pears, and either keep warm or chill in the refrigerator.

Return the juice to a brisk boil, and let it reduce and become slightly syrupy. Pour the sauce over the pears and serve.

PROFITEROLES WITH CHOCOLATE SAUCE

I honestly don't think that you can beat homemade profiteroles for a delicious, classic dessert!

Serves 6

INGREDIENTS
Choux Paste
1¼ cups water
⅓ cup butter
Pinch of salt
1½ cups all-purpose flour, sifted
5 large eggs, beaten

Chocolate Sauce
6 squares dark chocolate, melted
2 tablespoons superfine sugar
½ cup whipping cream

Filling
Scant 2 cups heavy cream,
   whipped

Preheat the oven to 425°F. Lightly grease two baking sheets. Bring the water to a boil in a saucepan, add the butter and the pinch of salt. Boil until the butter has melted. Remove the pan from the heat, and beat in the flour all at once. Beat until smooth – the paste will form a ball, and leave the sides of the pan. Gradually add the beaten egg, retaining a little for brushing, then use to fill a piping bag fitted with a plain tip. The paste should be smooth and glossy, and of a piping consistency.

Pipe 12 balls of choux paste onto the baking sheets. Mix the remaining beaten egg with a little water, and brush over the choux paste balls. Bake for 10 minutes; then reduce the heat to 350°F and bake for about an additional 20 minutes – the balls should double in size and be golden-brown. Remove from the oven, and pierce them to let the steam escape. Turn off the oven, and leave the door open. Put the profiteroles back into the open oven for about 10 minutes to dry out.

Melt the chocolate and sugar together in a bowl over a pan of boiling water, then stir in the whipping cream. Slice open the choux buns, and fill with the whipped cream. Pile up the buns in a serving dish or on a plate, and pour the chocolate sauce over to serve.

LEMON TART
TARTE AU CITRON

A few lemons grow in Provence but most of the French crop come from Corsica. This is a classic dessert from Provence, justly popular throughout France. Here is one method of preparing Tarte au Citron.

Serves 6

INGREDIENTS
Sweet Pastry Dough
2 cups all-purpose flour, sifted
Pinch of salt
½ cup butter, cut into cubes
½ cup sugar
1 egg, beaten

Lemon Filling
½ cup butter
¾ cup sugar
5 eggs, beaten
Juice of 2 lemons
Zest of ½ lemon

Preheat the oven to 375°F. Put the flour into a mixing bowl; add the salt, and rub in the butter. Stir in the sugar, then mix in the egg. Form the dough into a ball. Chill for 5-10 minutes. Roll out the dough on a floured counter, and use it to line a pie pan about 8 inches in diameter. Prick the dough bottom with a fork. Line the pie shell with baking parchment, and fill with baking beans, rice or dried beans. Bake for 15 minutes, then remove the beans and parchment. Return the pie shell to the oven for 5 minutes, or until the pastry is firm and golden.

Mix all the ingredients for the lemon filling in a saucepan. Put over a low heat, and stir continuously for 10 minutes. The mixture will become quite thick. Let cool, and chill slightly. Stir well, and then fill the pie shell. Keep the tart covered in the refrigerator until required.

CLAFOUTIS AUX CERISES

Clafoutis is usually made with tart, black cherries, but chopped prunes make an interesting variation. This traditional dessert is a thick sweet pancake-cum-batter pudding – delicious! Use canned cherries if necessary, but drain them thoroughly before use.

Serves 8

INGREDIENTS
½ cup butter
1¼ pounds fresh cherries
1 cup milk
Pinch of salt
½ cup superfine sugar
4 eggs, beaten
2 cups all-purpose flour, sifted

Preheat the oven to 350°F. Using a quarter of the butter, grease a large ovenproof dish. Spread the cherries in the bottom of the dish. Bring the milk to a boil, and add the salt; let cool slightly.

Melt the remaining butter, and mix in the sugar, eggs and flour. Pour the milk into the mixture, and mix well. Pour the batter over the cherries in the dish. Bake for about 50 minutes. Serve warm with cream.

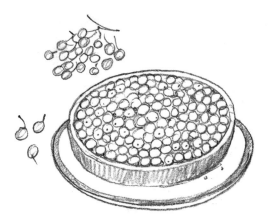

PEACHES IN RED WINE
PÊCHES AU VIN ROUGE

Peaches are one of the finest fruits grown in France, where there are many different varieties. They are delicious poached in red wine.

Serves 6

INGREDIENTS
2½ pints red wine
1½ cups sugar
1¼ cups water
1 stick cinnamon
1 vanilla bean
1 tablespoon finely chopped
  fresh lemon and orange zest
1 clove
6 firm peaches, peeled

Combine all the ingredients, except the peaches, in a large saucepan, and bring to a boil. Allow to boil until the syrup has reduced, and is slightly thickened. Place the peaches in the syrup, and poach them until they are cooked. Cooking time will depend on the quality and size of the peaches – test with the point of a sharp knife; there should be just a little resistance when cooked.

Remove the peaches from the syrup. Let the syrup cool slightly, and remove the clove, vanilla and the cinnamon.

Slice the peaches, and spread out into fan shapes on small individual plates. Pour the syrup over, and serve.

ÉCLAIRS

Éclairs are finger-shaped. They are traditionally filled with cream or crème pâtissière and frosted with chocolate, but many different fillings and toppings are used. I like coffee frosting for a change.

Makes 12

INGREDIENTS
Choux Paste
Scant 1 cup water
⅓ cup butter or margarine
¾ cup all-purpose flour, sifted
3 eggs

Filling
1¼ cups Crème pâtissière (see recipe)

Glacé Frosting
1 pound confectioners' sugar
Hot water
Few drops vanilla extract

Preheat the oven to 350°F. Combine the water and butter for the pastry in a deep saucepan and bring to a boil. Once boiling rapidly, take the pan off the heat. Stir in the flour all at once, and beat just until the mixture leaves the side of the pan. Spread out onto a plate to cool. When cool, return to the saucepan, and gradually add the beaten eggs. Beat well in between each addition of egg until the paste is smooth and shiny – it should be of soft dropping consistency, but holding its shape well. It may not be necessary to add all the egg.

Pipe or spoon the paste into strips about 3 inches long, spaced well apart on lightly greased baking sheets. Sprinkle the sheets lightly with water, and place in the oven. Immediately increase the oven temperature to 375°F. Make sure the paste is very crisp before removing it from the oven: this will take about 20-30 minutes. If the paste is not crisp, return it to the oven for an additional 5 minutes.

Sift the confectioners' sugar into a bowl and add hot water, stirring continuously until the mixture is of thick coating consistency. The frosting should cover the back of a wooden spoon but run off slowly. Add the vanilla extract.

To assemble the éclairs, cut the choux paste almost in half lengthwise and either pipe or spoon in the Crème Pâtissière. Using a large spoon, coat the top of each éclair with a smooth layer of glacé frosting. Let the frosting set before serving.

TARTE TATIN

An upside-down apple tart, created by two sisters named Tatin who ran a restaurant in the Loire valley. One of the most popular of French desserts.

Serves 6

INGREDIENTS
1 pound flaky pastry dough
2¼ pounds apples, peeled, halved and cored
⅓ cup butter
¾ cup superfine sugar
Whipped cream for serving

Preheat the oven to 450°F. Dot the base of a pie pan (about 8 inches in diameter) with the butter, and sprinkle with half the sugar. Place the apple halves, rounded side down, on the butter and sugar, and sprinkle with the remaining sugar. Roll the pastry dough out into a round just slightly larger than the bottom of the pan, and place it over the apples, tucking it down at the edges.

Bake for about 30 minutes. Remove from the oven, and invert immediately onto a serving plate. Serve hot with cream.

PRALINE MILLEFEUILLE

Pastry slices are often filled with cream and strawberries, but the praline-flavored confectioners' cream or custard makes a bitter-sweet filling which I actually prefer.

Serves 4

INGREDIENTS
1 cup milk
1 tablespoon crushed Praline (see recipe)
2 egg yolks
2½ tablespoons sugar
1½ tablespoons all-purpose flour, sifted
8 ounces puff pastry
Confectioners' sugar
Cocoa powder

Preheat the oven to 400°F, and slightly dampen a baking sheet. Boil the milk with the crushed praline. Beat the egg yolks with the sugar until pale and fluffy, then beat in the flour, mixing well. Pour the hot milk over the mixture; stir well, and pour back into the saucepan. Bring to a boil; then reduce the heat, and cook, stirring continuously, until the mixture thickens. Set aside to cool.

Roll the pastry dough out very thinly into a large rectangle, and place on a large baking sheet. Bake for 10 minutes until risen and golden. Remove from the oven, and let cool. Carefully cut the cooked, cooled pastry first into three long strips and then crosswise into 12 matching rectangles. Spread a little of the pastry cream over one of the rectangles, then cover with another rectangle of pastry, spread with more filling and finish with a third pastry rectangle. Continue until you have assembled four millefeuilles. Sift a little confectioners' sugar and cocoa over the top of the pastries to decorate.

KING'S CAKES
GALETTES DE ROIS

*These cakes are traditionally served at the feast of Epiphany.
A charm may be baked in the filling of one of the cakes in
the same way that a charm or a coin might be hidden in a
Christmas pudding.*

Serves 4

INGREDIENTS
¼ cup softened butter
4 tablespoons superfine sugar
1 egg, beaten
½ cup ground almonds
2 tablespoons Crème Pâtissière
  (see recipe)
1 teaspoon rum
1 pound puff pastry
1 egg, beaten

Preheat the oven to 450°F. Lightly grease a large baking sheet. Beat together the butter and sugar, then add the egg and ground almonds to make a thick almond cream. Beat in the crème pâtissière and the rum until thoroughly mixed.

Roll out the pastry dough thinly, and cut it into eight rounds, four of which should be slightly larger then the others. Place the four smaller rounds on the greased baking sheet, and prick them all over with a fork. Place the almond cream in a piping bag, fitted with a plain tip, and pipe the cream into the center of the rounds, leaving a wide margin all the way around the filling. Brush a little beaten egg around the edges of the dough rounds, then cover them with the larger rounds, pressing the edges together and crimping them to seal the galettes completely. Brush the tops with the remaining beaten egg to give the cooked galettes a glossy finish. Bake for about 20 minutes, until the galettes are golden-brown.

FRUIT MILLEFEUILLES

Assemble these at the last possible moment to keep them crisp. Use your favorite fresh fruits in season, and serve the fruit slices with a slightly sharp raspberry coulis. I think the ideal size for these millefeuilles is 4 × 2½ inches – substantial but not too big.

Serves 4

INGREDIENTS
12 ounces puff pastry
⅔ cup heavy cream
5 tablespoons Crème Pâtissière (see recipe)
1 teaspoon any orange liqueur
2 kiwi fruits
5 clementines

Preheat the oven to 400°F. Dampen two baking sheets. Roll out the pastry dough very thinly to fit the two dampened baking sheets. Prick all over with a fork, then bake for about 10-15 minutes, until browned. Whip the cream, and fold it into the crème patissière with the orange liqueur. Peel the kiwi fruits and slice them into rounds. Peel and segment the clementines, removing the skin from each segment.

Cut each cooled pastry sheet into six equal portions, making twelve in total. Divide the cream evenly between the twelve portions, spreading it smoothly. Decorate four with the clementine segments, and another four with the kiwi slices, reserving a little of each fruit for decorating the finished millefeuilles. Top each clementine portion first with a kiwi portion and then with a plain portion. Decorate each pastry with the reserved fruit, and serve.

FRENCH APPLE TURNOVERS

A classic recipe of Normandy, one of the main apple-growing areas of France. Cinnamon is the traditional seasoning, but I like to use ground mace with apples occasionally for a change.

Serves 4

INGREDIENTS
1 pound apples
3 tablespoons sugar
⅔ cup water
460g/1lb puff pastry
Cinnamon
1 egg, beaten

Preheat the oven to 400°F. Lightly grease a baking sheet. Peel, core and dice the apples. Put them into a saucepan with the sugar and water, and cook, stirring occasionally, until the water has evaporated. Use a fork to mash the apples to a smooth purée, and reserve about 6 tablespoons of this purée.

Roll out the dough but not too thinly, and cut out four large rounds. Place on the baking sheet, and prick them all over with a fork. Spoon 1½ tablespoons of apple purée over one half of each of the dough rounds. Sprinkle with cinnamon to taste. Brush beaten egg around the edges of each round. Fold each empty dough round half over the apple purée; press the edges together, and crimp them with your fingers to seal well and prevent leakage during cooking. Brush the turnovers with beaten egg. Bake for 20 minutes until golden-brown. Let cool slightly before serving.

PARIS-BREST

A Parisian specialty, originally created to celebrate the Paris to Brest cycle race. Small pastries make attractive individual servings but this dessert may also be made in a large round and sliced. The praline cream filling is essential.

Serves 4

INGREDIENTS

Choux Paste
½ cup water
2 tablespoons butter
1 teaspoon sugar
Pinch of salt
4 tablespoons all-purpose flour
2 eggs
1 tablespoon slivered almonds
Confectioners' sugar

Filling
1 cup heavy cream
4 tablespoons crushed Praline (see recipe)
4 tablespoons Crème Pâtissière (see recipe)

Preheat the oven to 400°F. Lightly grease a baking sheet. Put the water, butter, sugar and salt into a saucepan, and bring to a boil. When the butter has melted and the water is boiling, add the flour all at once. Beat continuously for a few minutes until the paste comes away cleanly from the sides of the pan and forms a ball. Remove the pan from the heat, and beat in the eggs one by one, reserving a little for glazing, to obtain a smooth dough suitable for piping. Spoon into a piping bag, fitted with a plain tip, and pipe four rings onto the greased baking sheet. Brush the paste with the reserved beaten egg, and sprinkle with the almonds. Bake for 20 minutes until golden brown. Remove the choux rings from the oven, and let them cool on a wire rack; then slice them in half horizontally.

To make the filling, whip the cream until stiff. Add the praline to the crème pâtissière, then fold in the whipped cream. Place the filling in a piping bag with a plain metal tip. Pipe the filling into the bottom half of the choux rings, then replace the tops. Sift confectioners' sugar over the pastries, and serve immediately.

AMANDINES

These are rich sweet tarts and may be made at any time of year. I think that they are typical winter "comfort" food.

Serves 4

INGREDIENTS
Half quantity sweet pastry, (see recipe)
¼ cup softened butter
4 tablespoons sugar
1 egg
1 cup ground almonds
2 tablespoons raspberry jam

Preheat the oven to 350°F. Roll out the dough, and use it to line four individual, greased pie pans. Set aside in the refrigerator.

Beat the butter and sugar together until pale; then add the egg, and continue to beat until completely mixed. Stir in the ground almonds to form a thick paste – add a little more if necessary. Spread the jam evenly over the bottom of the four pastry cases, and spoon or pipe the almond mixture carefully and evenly over the jam. Do not overfill the pie shells.

Bake the amandines for about 30 minutes. Let cool before removing from the pans.

BASIC RECIPES

The recipes contained within this chapter may seem like a rather odd assortment and, in truth, I suppose that they are! However, they are a collection of basic recipes without which no book on Classic French Cookery would be complete!

Basic Sauces

Here are the recipes for vinaigrette and mayonnaise, two salad dressings that are common to almost every western cuisine. There are many different ways of preparing both – if you don't get the flavor and seasoning quite right the first time, persevere until the dressing is to your liking. I usually use sugar in vinaigrette, but some people like to use honey – brown sugar will give a slightly richer flavor than white, and so the variations go on! I prefer to use lemon juice when making mayonnaise; others use wine vinegar. I assume that you will use Dijon mustard in the salad dressings – the yellow English mustard will work just as well but has a stronger, more pungent flavor. Aïoli, a rich garlic sauce somewhat similar to mayonnaise, is served with many French dishes, and a recipe is included elsewhere in this book. An easy recipe for Hollandaise, another sauce used extensively with fish and vegetables, is included here.

Sweet Success

There are two custard recipes that everyone should have at their fingertips in order to prepare a really diverse and successful range of sweet dishes. One is Crème Pâtissière, a rich, thick vanilla custard which is often used in place of cream as a filling for tarts and pies, and the other is an egg custard sauce. This bears no relationship at all to instant custard! In the new style of French cuisine, nouvelle cuisine, egg custard sauce is often served under tartlets or poached fruits, so as not to mask their appearance. Chocolate sauce or redcurrant jelly may be marbled through the sauce for extra effect.

Egg Dishes for Light Lunches

I have also included several egg dishes in this section, simply because they didn't seem to belong anywhere else! Pipérade is almost a Spanish omelet, whereas the Scrambled Eggs with Olives recipe belongs to the new style of French cookery, a development which is keeping the traditional cuisine alive. I have also included a recipe for Quiche Lorraine. Was there ever a dish that was so plagiarized and plundered? The original recipe hails from Alsace-Lorraine and should include bacon cooked in an egg custard within a pastry shell. Quiche should never be eaten hot – cutting the flan when it comes straight from the oven makes the filling separate and become watery – always serve quiche warm or cold. If you must add vegetables to the filling, cook them lightly, and drain off any juices that may come from them during cooking – these would make the pastry soggy, and may cause the filling to curdle.

Cookies and Cakes

The French are very good cooky makers, and even their commercially baked cookies are really quite special. There are three different cookies that are often served with coffee or with sorbets, mousses and other desserts: *tuiles d'amandes*, *langues de chats* and *palmiers*, all named because of their distinctive shapes. Even French commercial biscuits cannot compare in flavor to those made at home! They are all quite simple to make and to bake – shaping the *tuiles d'amandes* is the most complicated process, but a good supply of pencils will help with that. When shaping the cookies, move quickly – they have to be molded straight from the oven, or they will harden and set. Should that happen before you have shaped them, put the cookies back into the oven for just a couple of minutes on their baking sheet to soften again – no harm will come to them.

Cakes in France are often lighter than the traditional cakes of some other countries. For example, whisked sponges are always made rather than butter cakes. Fruit cakes are lighter as well, and are usually baked in *tranche* or loaf pans. I have simply run out of space, even in a collection of 200 recipes, to include much baking, but I have managed to squeeze in a *Gâteau Breton*, a Breton Butter Cake, which is almost a cross between a rich pastry and a cooky. It is delicious by itself, but is equally good served with fruit mousses and desserts, in a similar way to fingers of shortbread. Make sure that you use good unsalted butter for this recipe.

VINAIGRETTE OR FRENCH DRESSING

This dressing is used in so many different ways, as a salad dressing, hot over vegetables and as a seasoning. There are many recipes, but this is the way I like to make it, using the best of French ingredients.

Serves 4

INGREDIENTS
6 tablespoons extra virgin olive oil
2 tablespoons good wine vinegar
Salt and freshly ground black pepper
1 teaspoon Dijon mustard, or more to taste
Pinch of sugar
Freshly chopped mixed herbs or crushed garlic, (optional)

Put all the ingredients into a screw-topped jar or vinaigrette shaker, and shake until well blended. Taste carefully, and season as required. Herbs or garlic may be added for extra flavor. Use as required.

MAYONNAISE

This is probably the classic cold sauce in international cuisine. It is based on eggs and oil, so it is rich in flavor and calories! I actually don't like to use olive oil in mayonnaise – I find the flavor too strong, and prefer to use a sunflower or safflower oil.

Makes about 1¼ cups

Ingredients

3 egg yolks, or 1 whole egg plus
  one yolk
½ teaspoon dry mustard
Salt and white pepper
1 tablespoon wine vinegar or
  lemon juice
Pinch of sugar
1¼ cups sunflower oil

Put all the ingredients except the oil into a blender or food processor, and combine together briefly. Add the oil in a steady stream, with the machine running, and listen for the mayonnaise to thicken – it will sound deeper!

Season to taste and use as required.

QUICK HOLLANDAISE SAUCE

An easy way to produce a classic buttery sauce. This is excellent to serve with fish or vegetables.

INGREDIENTS
¾ cup butter
1 tablespoon wine or tarragon vinegar
2 tablespoons lemon juice
3 egg yolks
½ teaspoon superfine sugar
Pinch of salt
Pinch of cayenne pepper (optional)

Melt the butter slowly in a small saucepan, and, in another, heat the vinegar and lemon juice to boiling point. Put the egg yolks, sugar, salt and cayenne into a blender, and process for a few seconds. With the machine still running, very gradually add the vinegar and lemon juice mixture. When the butter has reached a boil, add this to the egg mixture in a slow drizzle, also with the machine running, until it is all incorporated and the sauce has thickened.

Serve at once, or keep warm by transferring it to a bowl placed over a saucepan of hot water.

SCRAMBLED EGGS WITH OLIVES

The addition of black olives to scrambled eggs turns this simple dish into a memorable one.

Serves 4

INGREDIENTS

12 eggs
4 tomatoes, seeded and chopped
15 black olives, pitted
½ cup olive oil
1 small onion, chopped
1 clove garlic, chopped
2 tablespoons butter
Salt and freshly ground black
   pepper

Beat the eggs, and set them aside. Chop the tomatoes and the olives together finely, using a blender or food processor. Warm the olive oil in a skillet, increase the heat to high, and cook the onion, garlic, tomatoes and olives until all the juices have evaporated.

Melt the butter in a large saucepan; add the beaten egg, and cook over a low heat, stirring continuously with a wooden spoon. Once the eggs are cooked, stir in the tomato mixture, and season to taste. Serve on small, warmed plates.

OMELETTE GOURMANDE

Omelet-making is an art, and, of course, the French are particularly good at it. Serve this large omelet sliced.

Serves 4

INGREDIENTS
4 onions, finely chopped
5 tablespoons oil
4 ounces mushrooms
12 eggs, beaten
1 tablespoon freshly chopped herbs
Salt and freshly ground black pepper

Sauté the onions in 2 tablespoons of oil over a high heat; then reduce the heat, and cook for an additional 20 minutes, until softened and lightly caramelized. In another large skillet, sauté the mushrooms in 1 tablespoon of the oil until soft. Remove from the heat. Add the beaten eggs to the mushrooms, and stir in half the onions. Cook over a high heat in as much of the remaining oil as necessary. Sprinkle with the herbs, and cook the omelet until the base is crisp but the filling is still slightly liquid. Fold one side of the omelet into the middle, then fold over the other side.

Serve on a bed of the remaining onions with a little salt and pepper. Serve sliced.

CHEESE SOUFFLÉ

Soufflés are popular throughout France. Many people worry about preparing hot soufflés, as they do collapse soon after cooking, so have everyone ready for the moment that the soufflé comes out of the oven.

Serves 6

INGREDIENTS
Butter for greasing
1½ cups grated cheese
2 tablespoons butter
¼ cup all-purpose flour
1¼ cups milk
Salt and freshly ground black
    pepper
Pinch of nutmeg
4 eggs, separated
1 extra egg white

Preheat the oven to 375°F. Grease a soufflé dish with butter, and scatter 3 tablespoons of the grated cheese inside it. Melt the butter in a heavy saucepan; whisk in the flour, and cook for about 1 minute. Gradually add the milk, and whisk continuously until the mixture thickens. Reduce the heat, and cook for 2 minutes. Add the salt and pepper, nutmeg and the egg yolks one by one, beating well with a wooden spoon. Let cool for about 5 minutes. Stir the remaining cheese into the white sauce. Beat the 5 egg whites until firm, then fold them gently into the cheese mixture with a metal spoon. Pour the mixture into the prepared soufflé dish, and bake for 40-45 minutes. The soufflé should be well risen and golden. Serve immediately.

QUICHE LORRAINE

The classic dish from the Lorraine region of France, in the northeast of the country. I once found a postcard of a quiche with a completely burned, black top to the filling – don't let yours overcook!

Serves 6-8

INGREDIENTS
Pastry Dough
1½ cups all-purpose flour
⅓ cup butter
Pinch of salt
½ egg, beaten with 1 tablespoon
  water

Filling
3 thick slices bacon, diced
4 eggs, beaten
½ cup milk
¾ cup heavy cream
Pinch of grated nutmeg
Salt and freshly ground black
  pepper

Preheat the oven to 375°F. To make the pastry dough, rub the butter into the flour with your fingertips until the mixture resembles fine bread crumbs. Add the salt, and bind the mixture together with the beaten egg and a little cold water. Chill for 5 minutes to rest.

Roll out the dough and use it to line a pie dish 7-8 inches in diameter. Dot the base of the pie with the diced bacon. Beat together the eggs, milk, cream, nutmeg and a little salt and pepper. Pour the egg mixture into the quiche, and bake immediately for 35-40 minutes. Serve warm or cold.

PISSALADIÈRE

You could describe this wonderful dish as a French pizza!
The topping is a rich mixture of caramelized onions with
thyme, anchovies and olives, cooked in the best traditions of
Provence, from where the recipe originates.

Serves 6

INGREDIENTS
2 pounds onions
Scant ½ cup extra virgin olive oil
2 fat cloves garlic, finely sliced
6-7 sprigs thyme
Salt and freshly ground black
    pepper
2 bay leaves
4 cups strong white bread flour
1 teaspoon sea salt
1 cake compressed fresh yeast
1 tablespoon sugar
2-ounce can anchovy fillets in
    olive oil, drained
Black olives for garnish

Peel and finely slice the onions. Heat 3 tablespoons of olive oil in a large skillet. Add the onions, and cook for 5 minutes, stirring once or twice. When the onions have started to reduce in volume, add the sliced garlic, salt and pepper, thyme and bay leaves. Cover the pan, and cook slowly for about 2 hours, until the onions have caramelized and cooked almost to a paste. Turn the onions into a strainer over a measuring jug, and let the juice drain into the jug.

Put the flour and sea salt together into a bowl, and make a well in the center. Add the remaining olive oil. Combine the yeast with the sugar. Measure the warm onion liquid, and make it up to 1 cup with water, adding a little to the yeast. Add the yeast and onion juice to the flour, and mix to a soft manageable dough. Knead on a lightly floured counter until smooth. Put the dough into a large mixing bowl, and cover. Leave in a warm place for 1 hour, until the dough has doubled in volume.

Scrape the dough from the bowl and knead it lightly again. Roll out to a rectangle to fit a large rectangular, lightly oiled baking sheet. Pull the dough to shape to fit into the corners. Leave, covered, for an additional 20 minutes to prove again.

Preheat the oven to 425°F. Brush the dough with a little olive oil, then spread it with the onion mixture, removing the thyme and bay leaves. Season with salt and pepper, and arrange the anchovy fillets and olives over the Pissaladière. Drizzle with extra olive oil.

Bake for 15-20 minutes. Cut into slices and serve immediately.

TARTE DE PROVENCE

A richly flavored tart that is ideal for summer eating. Serve warm or cold – this is excellent picnic food.

Serves 6

INGREDIENTS
Pastry Dough
1 cup self rising flour
¼ cup butter and white vegetable shortening, mixed
Cold water

Filling
1 pound ripe tomatoes
1 medium onion
1 tablespoon butter
Pinch of mixed herbs
2 tablespoons tomato paste
2 eggs, beaten
1 cup grated cheese
Salt and freshly ground black pepper
2-ounce can anchovy fillets
Black olives

Preheat the oven to 375°F. Prepare the dough by rubbing the fat into the flour and salt until the mixture resembles fine breadcrumbs. Mix to a firm dough with cold water. Roll out, and use to line a 8-inch quiche pan or porcelain flan dish. Chill until required.

Plunge the tomatoes into boiling water for a few seconds; remove and peel off the skins. Halve the tomatoes, and remove the seeds and cores. Chop the remaining flesh. Peel and finely chop the onion. Melt the butter in a large saucepan, and add the tomatoes, onion, herbs and tomato paste. Cover the pan, and cook over a low heat for 30 minutes until the mixture is reduced to a rich pulp. Take off the heat, and let cool for a minute or so; then beat in the eggs, cheese and seasoning. Pour this mixture into the prepared flan case, and garnish with a lattice of anchovy fillets, and dot with halved, pitted black olives. Bake above the center of the oven for 40 minutes until risen. (Always place a porcelain or china dish on a preheated baking sheet to conduct the heat, and insure that the underneath of the pastry is well cooked.) Serve warm or cold.

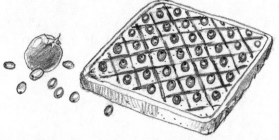

PIPÉRADE

A dish from the Pyrenées, an omelet showing Spanish influence in its use of bell peppers and tomatoes. Some people add tomato paste, others slices of Jambon de Bayonne (Bayonne ham). Do not overcook the omelet – it will toughen the eggs and spoil the dish.

Serves 2–4

INGREDIENTS

4 eggs
Salt and freshly ground black pepper
1 tablespoon freshly chopped marjoram and thyme
1 tablespoon olive oil
1 medium onion, chopped
1 medium green bell pepper, seeded and chopped
1 clove garlic, crushed
2 tomatoes, skinned, seeded and sliced
2 tablespoons butter

Crack the eggs into a bowl, and beat thoroughly with the salt, pepper and herbs.

Heat the oil in a skillet, and add the chopped onion, green bell pepper and garlic. Fry gently until soft but not brown. Add the tomatoes, and cook for an additional 3 minutes. Remove from the heat, and add to the egg mixture.

Melt the butter in the skillet, and, when frothing, add the omelet mixture. Cook slowly until the underside is golden-brown. Slide out onto a plate, and return to the skillet on the reverse side. Cook for a minute or two more. Do not overcook.

Serve hot immediately, or let cool completely, and cut into wedges for a picnic or cold buffet.

CARAMEL

This is a basic recipe for use in so many desserts. Sometimes different quantities of sugar and water will be given in an individual recipe, but the basic method of making a caramel is always the same.

INGREDIENTS
¾ cup granulated or superfine
  sugar
4 tablespoons cold water

Put the sugar and water into a small saucepan, and heat very gently until the sugar is dissolved – you do not want the mixture to boil until the sugar has dissolved. Stir well.

Bring the mixture to a boil, and boil rapidly until the caramel is a light golden color – do not stir while the caramel is boiling. Use immediately, or plunge the base of the pan into cold water to prevent the caramel from cooking on and burning. Use quickly.

PRALINE

Praline is a nutty caramel, usually left to harden and then crushed or ground before use. It is most commonly made with hazelnuts or almonds. The nuts are usually left in their skins for extra color, but may be blanched if preferred.

INGREDIENTS

4 ounces hazelnuts or almonds, toasted if wished
¾ cup granulated or superfine sugar
4 tablespoons cold water

Roughly chop the nuts, and put them on a thick, lightly greased baking sheet. Put the sugar and water into a small saucepan, and heat very gently until the sugar is dissolved – you do not want the mixture to boil until the sugar has dissolved. Stir well.

Bring the mixture to a boil, and boil rapidly until the caramel is a light golden color – do not stir while the caramel is boiling. Pour over the nuts, and leave to set until hard.

Crush the praline into small pieces – this is easiest to do with the end of a rolling pin. The praline may be ground finely in a pestle and mortar. Use as required.

EGG CUSTARD SAUCE

A classic vanilla-flavored sauce. It is used to pour over desserts or, in a more stylish cuisine, is often served under food, as a bed of sauce. For special occasions make the custard with heavy cream!

Serves 4

INGREDIENTS
6 egg yolks
2 tablespoons superfine sugar
1 teaspoon cornstarch
2½ cups milk
Few drops vanilla extract

Beat the egg yolks, sugar and cornstarch together lightly. Bring the milk almost to a boil, then pour it onto the egg mixture, beating constantly. Rinse the pan.

Return the custard to the pan, and put over a very low heat, stirring continuously, until the sauce starts to thicken, and will coat the back of a wooden spoon. Use as required.

CRÈME PÂTISSIÈRE

This recipe will make just over 1¼ cups of crème pâtissière or confectioners' custard. I often use this as a filling for fruit tarts – it is creamy but not too rich.

INGREDIENTS
1¼ cups milk
Vanilla bean or a few drops
  vanilla extract
3 egg yolks
¼ cup superfine sugar
2 tablespoons cornstarch
1 tablespoon butter

Pour the milk into a saucepan, and add the vanilla bean. Bring to a boil; then remove from the heat, and let infuse for about 20 minutes. Whisk together the egg yolks, sugar and cornstarch until thick and creamy. Add vanilla extract at this stage if you have not used a vanilla bean. Remove the bean from the milk, and slowly pour the liquid over the egg yolk mixture, stirring continuously. Rinse out the saucepan, and return the mixture to it. Stir vigorously over a low heat until the custard becomes thick. Transfer it to a bowl, and beat in the butter. Let cool. Cover with plastic wrap or baking parchment until needed. The crème pâtissière can be flavored with a little liqueur, or lightened by the addition of whipped cream.

SWEET PASTRY DOUGH

This is a classic pastry used for many sweet dishes and flans – it is often called a pâte sablé. It is richer than shortcrust pastry, and is made with self-rising flour. The pastry should be baked in an oven no hotter than 375°F, because of the high proportion of sugar which will cause the pastry to brown quickly.

INGREDIENTS
4 cups self-rising flour
⅔ cup butter
⅔ cup superfine sugar
3 eggs, beaten

Put the flour into a large bowl, and rub in the butter until the mixture resembles fine bread crumbs. Stir in the sugar, then add the beaten eggs, and bind the dough together using your hands.

Knead gently on a lightly floured counter, then wrap in plastic wrap or foil, and chill until required.

PALMIERS

Palmiers are sweet, crisp pastry cookies, deriving their shape from a process whereby the ends of the pastry are rolled toward the center forming attractive double curls. These cookies are best served on the day that they are made. Use superfine sugar or confectioners' sugar to dredge the cookies.

Serves 4-6

INGREDIENTS
8 ounces puff pastry
3 tablespoons superfine sugar
  plus sugar for dredging

Preheat the oven to 400°F. Lightly grease a baking sheet. Roll the pastry dough out to form a thin rectangle. Sprinkle the counter with half the sugar, and place the dough on the sugared surface; then sprinkle it with the remaining sugar. Lightly press the dough, so that the sugar sticks to it. Roll the two ends of the dough toward the middle, and place the rolled dough in the freezer for 20 minutes, to make it easier to slice.

Remove the dough from the freezer, and slice it thinly to form the curled cookies. Place them on a dampened baking sheet, and bake for 20 minutes, or until golden-brown. Let the cookies cool, then sprinkle them with extra sugar before serving.

ALMOND TILE COOKIES
TUILES D'AMANDES

These almond cookies are the perfect accompaniment to ice creams and mousses. Larger cookies should be molded over a rolling pin, while smaller cookies can be shaped over wooden pencils. They are named after the curved terracotta roof tiles popular throughout France.

Makes 30 cookies

INGREDIENTS
½ cup superfine sugar
2 egg whites
½ cup all-purpose flour
½ cup melted butter
¾ cup ground almonds
Extra butter for greasing

Preheat the oven to 400°F. Lightly grease some baking sheets. Beat the sugar into the egg whites, then add the flour and butter, beating well. Beat in the almonds, then let the mixture rest for 10 minutes.

Put spoonfuls of mixture onto the prepared baking sheets, allowing space for the cookies to spread, and bake each sheet for 3-4 minutes. Remove the cookies from the sheets with a spatula, and immediately shape them around a wooden pencil. They will cool and harden very quickly. Slide onto a wire rack to cool. Repeat the cooking and cooling operation until all the cookie batter has been used.

LANGUES DE CHAT

No langues de chat can ever compare in flavor to the homemade version. Use a ½ inch tip to pipe the cookies onto the baking sheets, and store the cooked cookies in an airtight tin.

Serves 6

INGREDIENTS
⅔ cup softened butter
2 cups superfine sugar
½ teaspoon vanilla extract
5 egg whites
2 cups all-purpose flour, siftd

Preheat the oven to 425°F. Lightly grease two baking sheets. Beat the butter and sugar until pale and fluffy, then add the vanilla extract. Add the egg whites one by one, alternating with the flour, until a fine dough is obtained.

Place the dough in a piping bag with a plain tip and pipe 3-inch strips of mixture onto the greased baking sheets. Leave space between the biscuits as they spread during baking. Bake for 10-15 minutes: the edges of the cookies should be golden-brown but the centers still pale.

Let the cookies cool slightly on the baking sheet, then use a palette knife to lift them onto a wire rack to cool completely.

BRETON BUTTER CAKE
GÂTEAU BRETON

This rich, buttery cake is a cross between a shortbread, a sponge cake and a rich pastry. Serve with a fruit pudding or eat it by itself.

Serves 8

INGREDIENTS
6 egg yolks
1 cup less 2 tablespoons unsalted
   butter, at room temperature
¾ cup superfine sugar
2¼ cups all-purpose flour

Preheat the oven to 325°F. Beat the egg yolks together in a bowl, then reserve a little of the egg in a small container. Add the softened butter to the egg yolks, and beat until soft and well blended. Add the sugar and flour, and work into a slightly sticky dough.

Lightly butter a 9-inch loose-bottomed cake pan. Press the dough into the pan, smoothing the top with a palette knife. Score into diamonds across the top with a fork, then brush with the reserved egg yolk. Bake for 50 minutes. Cool slightly before transferring to a wire rack.

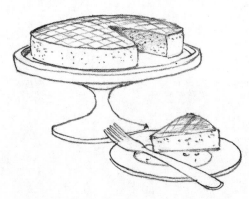

PETS DE NONNE

These little pastry balls are slightly sweet and very crisp. Serve immediately after baking, tossed in confectioners' sugar and cinnamon, with strong coffee or tea, as a midmorning or afternoon snack.

INGREDIENTS
⅔ cup water
2 tablespoons butter
Pinch of salt
1 teaspoon superfine sugar
4 tablespoons all-purpose flour
2 eggs, beaten
Oil for deep-frying
Confectioners' sugar and
  cinnamon

Bring the water to a boil in a saucepan with the butter, salt and sugar. When the water is boiling, add all the flour at once, and beat the mixture vigorously. Continue to beat for 1 minute over a low heat. Remove the saucepan from the heat, and beat in the first egg. When this is completely incorporated, beat in the second egg to obtain a smooth, elastic dough.

Heat the oil for deep-frying in a deep pan. Place the dough in a piping bag fitted with a plain metal tip. When the oil is hot, about 375°F, pipe small balls of dough onto a palette knife, dipped in the hot oil, then use a second palette knife to slide the balls off into the hot oil. Turn the pets de nonne during cooking, so that they cook evenly all over. Cook until puffed and golden-brown. Using a draining spoon, remove the pets de nonne. Drain on paper towels, and serve them immediately, sprinkled with sifted confectioners' sugar and cinnamon.

Index

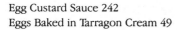